The A TO Z GUIDE for LIGHTWEIGHT TRAVELLERS

Clive Tully

Writer's BLOCK

Copyright © 1988 Clive Tully
Cartoons by Bill Stott

First published in the UK 1988 by Writer's Block, Butler House,
Norwich Road, Mulbarton, NR14 8JT

British Library Cataloguing in Publication Data

Tully, Clive
    The A to Z guide for lightweight travellers
    1. Travel
    I. Title
    910.4

    ISBN 0-9513410-0-6

Design by Lorna Tully
Typeset by Wordstream Ltd., Wordstream House, St. Adhelms
Road, Poole, Dorset, BH13 6BS
Printed and bound in Great Britain by Cambridge University
Press, University Printing House, Shaftesbury Road, Cambridge,
CB2 2BS

CONTENTS

How to use this book: The idea of the book is to give the traveller a speedy source of reference, the principle being that you shouldn't have to plough through an entire chapter on health care to find out what you need in your First Aid kit. Many of the entries in the A to Z are cross-referenced, so to read fully on one particular subject, such as photography, you would have to read the sections on photography, cameras, film and X-rays. Where appropriate, the A to Z also directs you to the appendices at the back of the book.

THANK YOU SO MUCH

Most books don't usually happen without the welcome interference or influence of others, and this one is no exception. Thanks first of all to my old friend, fellow traveller and drinking partner David Oswin, who unwittingly inspired this opus. David also came up with the amusing, if somewhat macabre, tale of the man who flew home in his own suitcase. Thanks too to Andrew Denton for contributing his experience of hitch-hiking.

Most authors write and re-write until they're cross-eyed, so it's always handy to have someone else to read through your manuscript, and ask you whether you really meant to qwrte from nasz6 Yrāh%(. And whilst a computer spelling checker sorts out all the minor mistakes, it isn't quite so hot on more complex matters. So thanks to my mum, who was still smiling after ploughing right through my first draft.

And lastly, thanks to Paul Howcroft. His Rohan lightweight clothes are without doubt the best designed for travellers, and it's not often you'll see me wearing anything else. Paul contributed sections on travelling with children, and safety, and his comments on the rest of the text have been invaluable. His enthusiasm, and (let's not beat about the bush here) money have helped turn this book, and our own publishing venture, from the uncertain haze of an idea into a reality.

Clive Tully

INTRODUCTION

Modern modes of travel make it simple for anyone to cover vast distances with relative ease. You could argue that much of the romance of travel to distant shores has suffered because of it. Victorian Englishmen were great travellers, but look at the way they used to undertake their voyages — chests packed with everything you could possibly imagine, probably including the kitchen sink! And why not live in style, when you have an army of porters and servants to fetch and carry for you? Well, it might have been good enough for wealthy Victorians, but I can't imagine that cushioned and cosseted by their imported home comforts, they ever experienced the true fascination of foreign travel, which must surely be the sole reason for going in the first place!

These days, armies of servants and huge piles of baggage no longer have any place in travelling for pleasure. Even the mountaineers who conquered the world's highest and most difficult peaks have scorned the siege tactics which placed human feet onto virgin summits. Where once there would have been mountains of equipment, scores of porters, and climbers working up some Himalayan mountain in relays to service a whole string of camps, they now use the fast-moving lightweight style of climbing developed in the Alps, to present a fairer and more intriguing challenge.

For the humble traveller, the free baggage allowance of 20 kilos available for the majority of international flights really ought to be about as much as you'd ever want to carry. Indeed, it's quite possible to clothe and equip yourself for a trip of several weeks with considerably less.

In the last few years, a revolution in lightweight clothing has enabled the dedicated traveller to pursue the ultimate dream — to take everything he needs in one modest package, which can travel either as a shoulder bag or rucksack, small enough to perch on the luggage rack of a bus, and small enough to travel as cabin luggage on aeroplanes. No more exertion, dragging suitcases from one place to another, and no stress at the baggage reclaim, waiting and hoping that your suitcase arrived safely.

Today's lightweight traveller does it differently. A couple of changes of clothing sit comfortably in a small rucksack or shoulder bag — clothing which, despite its light weight, is rugged enough to take the strain of modern travel, and in a wide variety of conditions. And considering that it's possible to get on an aircraft in cold, wet London, and get off again in a matter of hours in temperatures considerably warmer, travel clothes with the versatility to handle a wide range of conditions makes life a lot more enjoyable.

The A to Z Guide is intended for people travelling light. It follows that the independent traveller may be going right off the beaten track, possibly on foot or two wheels, so there are comprehensive sections on the important aspects of camping equipment, rucksacks, keeping your feet in shape, and lots more tips not covered by the run-of-the-mill travel guides.

To an extent, my travelling luggage isn't as light as it could be. The tools of my trade are a bag of cameras and lenses, and a portable computer, all of which add weight with which most travellers are fortunate enough not to be burdened. But without the benefits of weight savings in the rest of my luggage, journeys would be rather tiresome. So, ditch all those old-fashioned ideas, and read on to find out how you become a lightweight traveller.

Note: This book is probably unique in another respect. Not only is it a book **about** travel, a fair proportion of it was actually written **whilst** travelling! The lynchpin of the operation was an Epson PX8 battery operated portable computer. The PX8 is the ideal machine for the travelling writer — mine has rattled across the northern fringes of the Sahara on the top of a Land Rover. It has been bumped about in a cycle saddle bag, and has been subjected to all manner of treatment probably never envisaged by the manufacturers, and it still works! Above all, it has made many long hours on trains 'n boats 'n planes 100% productive.

ACCOMMODATION

ACCOMMODATION – *See Youth Hostels, Camp Sites*

If you plan to stay in hotels, or youth hostels in popular areas, you'll stand a better chance of getting what you want by booking ahead. Otherwise, you just have to take pot luck. Even camp sites can fill up, so don't take any chances if you've set your heart on a particular place. On the other hand, the independent traveller might actually prefer the spice of not knowing where he might be staying each night. And if you're not too bothered about what sort of place you rest your head in, it's unlikely that you won't be able to find somewhere to stay.

Having said that, I've been amassing my own special collection of places in which I've snoozed over the last few years. They include sleeping on a variety of floors, **on** someone's dining table, in a ditch, tents, bothies, barns, buses, trains, boats and planes – oh, and five star hotels!

AIRLINE FARES

The different fares available from airlines can be somewhat confusing at a first look. These are the different types of ticket available.
Round the world: Quite commonly available now, usually with small groups of airlines working together to provide particular routes. They offer the option of travelling either east or west, with no backtracking allowed. You can usually stop over in several places, although the numbers of stops and other restrictions vary from one airline to another.
Apex/Super Apex: Advance Purchase Excursion tickets have to be booked at least a fortnight in advance, and often longer. They are return tickets only, without stop-overs, and minimum stays are usually specified. Super Apex tickets are cheaper, but only become available at the last moment, if at all.
Pex/Super Pex: Available for European flights, over the counter Economy Class tickets for immediate use. They sometimes include a compulsory Saturday night stay at your destination.
Excursion fares: Just like the British Rail Saver ticket, really. A reduced fare ticket for scheduled routes, but with restrictions on the times of travel. Travel must be on the days and times specified, otherwise you become liable to pay the full fare.
Spouse Fares: Available mainly in Europe from the larger airlines, although generally declining as a scheme. It allows one spouse 50% off provided the other pays the full fare. Couples may have to prove they are married, and must travel together on both

legs of the journey to qualify.

ITX Fares: Inclusive Tour Excursion fares, like Spouse fares, are becoming less popular with the big airlines. Available as part of a holiday package which includes hotel accommodation, although you can get some covering just the flight, and no accommodation. Generally complicated restrictions on the length of stay.

Student/Youth Fares: Available to young people under the age of 22, but with some leeway for older people still in full-time education. Discounts vary, but are usually something like 25%.

Standby Fares: Discount tickets which can be bought if there are seats remaining on a flight which haven't been sold. They're available up to the final check-in time before the flight leaves, and any unsold seats are allocated to standby ticket holders on the basis of first come, first served. Can be a cheap way to travel, but with no certainty as to whether you can get a seat on a particular flight, not much use if your trip has to keep to a timetable.

Scheduled Consolidation Fares: Similar to ITX, in that they have a minimum stay restriction, Scheduled Consolidation Fares are blocks of tickets which the airlines sell to various operators at charter prices.

Air Passes: Sold under such titles as Air Rover, these passes allow discount air travel within a specific country. Usually valid for a specified period, they will be restricted to a maximum number of stops.

ALARM CLOCK/WATCH

It's almost inevitable that at some point during your trip, you're going to have to make the supreme sacrifice, and wrench yourself from the arms of Morpheus at some ungodly hour, either to get to a port of departure, or to wake you up in time on a train to get off at the right station. The human body clock is actually quite reliable. If you keep telling yourself before you go to bed that you need to get up at 6 am, you almost invariably wake up just before. It doesn't work so well for everyone, so some kind of fail-safe is advisable, especially when you've recently travelled to another time zone, and your body clock (more correctly known as circadian rhythms) will be out of step.

Some hotels have computerised telephone systems which enable you to programme your own alarm call, set off by the telephone ringing. You can, of course, book an alarm call at reception, although I've found from bitter experience that such things can't always be relied on. Travelling quartz alarm clocks with liquid crystal screens are very light and compact, and can usually be bought for under £10. If you have an alarm wrist watch, make sure yours will actually rouse you when you need it. Some watch alarms make the puniest noise imaginable, and wouldn't wake anyone not endowed with the auricular attributes of a dog or bat.

ALCOHOL

Great stuff at the right time, and in the right place. Airline cabin crews tempt you with plenty of it when you're in- flight, and it's probably one of the worst things you can do, particularly on a long-haul flight. Flying tends to dehydrate you, because you're breathing dry air, and with the cabin pressure at the equivalent altitude of 9,000 feet or so, the last thing you want is alcohol, which merely serves to dehydrate you more.

Although some duty free booze is becoming available in unbreakable plastic bottles, it's interesting to note that very few airports offer duty free facilities for incoming passengers. You could argue that the rule about passengers not being allowed to carry flammable liquids is made a mockery of when passengers are each permitted to carry a litre of whisky, brandy or vodka on board. A forced landing, with two or three hundred litres of highly flammable spirit crashing about the cabin apparently isn't considered dangerous.

If you're driving abroad, take extra special care with the booze. Court cases here over the last few years have shown that it is quite literally possible for a drunken driver to get away with murder. You won't be as lucky in foreign parts, because a good few countries allow drivers no leeway at all with alcohol. Whatever your stance on the subject, don't forget that driving down unfamiliar roads in a foreign country gives you more than enough to concentrate on. Penalties for driving even with the tiniest bit of alcohol in your blood in Scandinavian countries are severe — if you get nobbled by the law, I won't have the slightest bit of sympathy for you.

Consider also when and where you consume your alcohol in relation to the company you keep. Whilst some Muslims are becoming more lax on such matters, it's still against the law in many countries. If you start indulging in drunken parties in a 'dry' area, be prepared for the consequences! Lastly, and disappointingly, no doubt, a swig from the hip flask will not warm you up. Neither does it cure any ills (other than alleviating the imagined ones in a most pleasant manner). Read medicinal as 'medicinal'!

ALTITUDE SICKNESS

Most of us (in the UK, at least) live somewhere between sea level and 1,000 feet above. Once you move beyond 7 or 8,000 feet, things have to slow down, simply because the air is thinner, and consequently there isn't so much oxygen. Aircraft cabins are generally pressurised to the equivalent of 9,000 feet, which is about as low as they can take it before you really start to notice it. Even so, you might have some adjustment problems like popping ears. On the ground, particularly if you're trekking or climbing, it takes time to acclimatise to altitude. Your body needs to manufacture more red blood corpuscles to make better use of the available oxygen. I know someone who, recognising this fact, decided to hit the cigarettes with a vengeance, and smoke like a chimney prior to setting out on a Himalayan trip. No doubt it increased his red corpuscle count, but at what cost?

The reaction to altitude varies from one person to another, and it doesn't necessarily mean that the youngest and fittest is least likely to suffer. I've experienced the symptoms of mild altitude sickness, and even that wasn't something I'd recommend. I'd climbed about 1,200 feet from 11,500, virtually non-stop, and at a pace more fitting for a 1,200 foot ascent in the Lake District. What I should have done was take it slowly, stopping for frequent five minute rests. As it was, I showed the classic symptoms of headache, nausea, feeling perpetually cold, and being unable to sleep. I was prescribed a diuretic to stave off the fluid retention problems which altitude sickness also brings, and found myself suffering from a dose of the trots as well.

The next day, I descended several thousand feet, and apart from feeling exhausted, suffered no further ill effects. Severe altitude sickness leads to pulmonary or cerebral oedema, where fluid builds up in the lungs or around the brain. This situation is potentially fatal, and must be corrected by an immediate and rapid descent to a safe altitude.

ATTITUDE

Not everyone has the same outlook on life as you. There will be points during your travels where you may be harassed, ignored, subjected to zealous bureaucracy or sheer incompetence. Not everyone will jump when you snap your fingers or raise your voice, and despite your heartfelt protestations of abject poverty, others may regard you as a bottomless pit of money, and therefore look upon you as fair game.

Whatever the problem, it's best by far not to get

into a flap about it, or at least not to let the other person see you're bothered. By all means be firm if the situation demands it, but keep it polite, and you stand a better chance of resolving things than by losing your temper. A smile in the face of all known horrors can be disarming enough to win the day. Patience, and a flexible attitude, will see you through most travelling problems.

BAGGAGE

BAGGAGE – *See also Rucksacks, Check-in, Insurance*

How much baggage do you travel with? If you get to the end of this book, and you still find yourself approaching 20 kilos with your luggage, you're doing something wrong! Air travellers can get around the possibility of paying excess baggage fares by checking in their luggage with someone else, hopefully with a little more sense.

But you really shouldn't need to pinch a bit of someone else's free baggage allowance. Apart from the fact that it can get darned heavy to lug around, there's more to go wrong. Strictly speaking, your free baggage allowance should include your cabin baggage. In practice, it's very rare that it gets weighed. Perhaps I shouldn't admit it here, but my tiny cabin bag crammed full of photographic equipment and portable computer often weighs more than my checked-in baggage! The usual rule is that cabin baggage should conform to certain dimensions to fit under the seat in front of you. Generally, the sum of the length, width and height of the bag should not exceed 45 inches, the maximum dimensions being 20 by 15 by 10 inches.

BICYCLE

The best bike for lightweight travellers is a good quality touring bike. It's possible to get by on a racing bike, or even the sort of thing more suitable for commuting, but you'll certainly feel the difference once you start riding longer distances. The technicalities of different bikes is beyond me, and, so it seems to me, beyond a lot of the experts. There always seems to be lively debate in the pages of the cycling press as to what's good, and what isn't. Certainly, if you've got plenty of money to spend, you won't have any trouble getting rid of it all buying a quality bike with all the most expensive components. But for those of more modest means, I would suggest £200 to £300 should buy a reasonable bike, and £500 will buy a very good one.

Frames come in the men's diamond shape, or the ladies' mixte. Whilst the mixte shape makes it easier for a lady wearing a skirt to step through the frame with modesty, rather than hoicking one leg over the saddle to get on and off, it does have the disadvantage of being less rigid. Nowhere is this more apparent than when the bike is loaded up with panniers, and you get out of the seat to give yourself a bit more power pedalling up a hill. The bike loses stability, feeling as though the back end is attached to the front by a hinge. Many women cyclists cast conventional attitudes aside, and ride diamond frame bikes.

The best lightweight frames have double butted tubing, which means that if you took sections of the tube at various points along its length, you'd find each end thickest, tapering to thinner metal in the middle. Reynolds 531 is generally regarded as the best frame tubing.

Like a pair of shoes, the size of the frame is all-important, as a poor fit will manifest itself in all manner of aches and pains once you hit the open road. There are several ways of determining the right size. Subtracting nine inches from your inside leg measurement gives you your frame size, as does measuring your height in inches and dividing by three. You should be able to stand astride the cross-bar of a diamond frame bike comfortably, feet flat on the ground. The saddle is at the correct height when your leg is stretched out straight with the arch of your foot on the pedal at its lowest point.

Detailing the rest of the components of a bike is getting rather specialised, and it's only the real fanatic who painstakingly selects the individual components of his choice to build his perfect bicycle. Good quality off-the-shelf hand-built tourers are available for £300 to £500. The Raleigh Classic models fall into this category, as do Orbit and Eclipse.

Having said that, my own bicycle is a little more unusual, a Moulton AM7. It has ten inch wheels, a low slung multi-tube 'space' frame which comes apart at the middle, and suspension front and rear. It's a superb bike for touring, very light and responsive, and holes, cobbles and ruts are all gobbled up effortlessly by the suspension. Whatever type of bike you settle on, make sure you have the essential tools, puncture repair kit, and a few spares like inner tube and spokes, before setting off on the great trek.

A bike makes a great way of getting about, but it does need some thought beforehand if you plan to take it on any form of public transport. You can usually park it in the guard's van on a British train, although the Intercity ones usually need advance booking, as space is limited. Peak Intercity services may refuse to take bicycles. Depending on which service you use, you may have to pay. Remove all your luggage from the bike once in the guard's van, and it's also best to have a label somewhere showing your name and destination.

Most ferry companies take bicycles at not much more than the foot passenger rate, although it pays to stay with your bike whilst the crew member on the car deck secures it. The paint job on your luxury tourer might look a little the worse for wear if you allow some deck hand to lash heavy rope around the frame without any thought of protection.

When you transport your bike by air, it's best to

find out in advance what the airline's requirements are. Some don't take bikes, and others may not make any specific provisions to cover against rough handling. In most situations, you'll be asked to turn the pedals inside out, turn the handlebars round sideways, and deflate the tyres.

Quality airlines provide large plastic crates for bicycles, so they won't suffer from the inevitable heavy handed treatment, and to make it easier for them to fit it in with all the other baggage. Nevertheless, I know people who've collected their bicycles at the other end of a flight to discover their beloved machines reduced to twisted, mangled wrecks. Unfortunately, the compensation for damage which you're likely to receive from the airline isn't likely to reflect the true value of the bike, so adequate insurance is the order of the day.

BINOCULARS

A small pair of bins can be handy things to have with you, even if you aren't an ardent bird-watcher. I'm no twitcher, but I do appreciate a close-up view of the wildlife, especially if it's particularly colourful. When I'm out in the wilds, my miniature binoculars come into their own for route-finding. It makes navigation a lot easier if you can spy out such things as river crossing points, the safest route across dodgy ground, and anything else where your chances can be improved by deciding before you actually get into the area.

I use a small pair of folding 8x20 binoculars, and there are several makes around which you can pick up for £50 to £60. You can get 10x magnification models, but I find they're just that bit more difficult to hold still. 8x is certainly good enough for general use. The extremely wealthy might like to go for the superlative excellence of Leitz binoculars, but I shan't mention prices — I hate to see grown people cry!

BITES AND STINGS — *See also Insect Repellent*

At the very least, irritating, and at worst, a serious setback to your travel plans. As always, prevention is the best line of defence. Use insect repellent, and cover up exposed skin at dusk, when the mozzies become more active. Other biters and stingers include snakes, spiders, scorpions, bees, hornets, jellyfish, stingrays and other poisonous fish.

Snakes and scorpions, like most other creatures, won't tangle with you unless you leave them no option. The vibrations through the ground as you tramp along will be enough to send them scuttling for cover. But if you happen to take them by surprise, they may well defend themselves.

If you get stung by a bee, don't use tweezers to remove the stinger, as it may squeeze more poison into you. Use a needle to remove it instead. A cold compress may relieve some of the pain, and anti-histamine tablets can help reduce the irritation.

The old wild west films always used to show the hero dramatically slashing the hapless snake bite victim's wound, sucking and then spitting out blood and venom. Surprisingly, some still think this is the way to deal with them!

The American made Sawyer Snake Bite Extractor is a useful piece of kit, basically a powerful suction pump, with four different sized heads to cater for bites of different sizes, nicely packaged in an unbreakable plastic box. It works by applying a strong suction force to the area of skin around the bite or sting, enough to bring any poison out through the punctures that were made to let it in.

By removing poison from the injury without speeding its entry into your bloodstream, the extractor can help even with a minor insect bite or sting, particularly if you suffer with allergic reactions to such things. More importantly, it can save your life if you're unfortunate enough to be bitten by a dangerously venomous snake.

BIVVY BAGS – *See also Sleeping Bags*

A waterproof sleeping bag cover weighing just 1½ pounds may sound very attractive to anyone keen on keeping weight and packed bulk to a minimum. Gore-Tex has made bivvying almost as comfortable as camping with a tent. If anything, the material works better in a bivvy bag. The smaller enclosed space means that it can more easily build up the moisture differential required to make the material work properly. The Gore-Tex bivvy bag fits generously over a sleeping bag, and a large hood takes care of equipment storage. Most have a zipped entrance across the bag, at about shoulder height, with a Velcro fastened weather flap to keep the weather from penetrating the zip. Not having that ghastly condensation problem makes things much more tolerable. Your sleeping bag performs as it should, and you're not reduced to putting all your belongings in plastic bags to keep them dry.

Gore-Tex bivvy bags are available from quite a number of manufacturers, and apart from minor details, they're pretty much the same. The vast majority are available in olive green, a nice unobtrusive colour.

BIVVY BAGS

'I don't want to be around when that turns into a butterfly!'

Around £50 to £70 should buy you one with tape sealed seams (most important).

A bivvy bag is also a very good means of uprating a sleeping bag for use in a tent in colder weather. Used like this, it should extend the range of your bag by around 10 degrees C. You don't even need an uprated sleeping bag for bivvying. You aren't in any less shelter than you would be in a tent, and in fact you're likely to be warmer, so stick to what you would normally for any particular season. If you use a down bag, and the weather looks as though it might turn bad, you'd do well to keep the sleeping bag in situ, packing the whole lot into a plastic bag in your rucksack.

CAMERA – See also Photography, Film, X-Rays

What sort of camera do you use for travelling? It depends on how important taking pictures is to you. If all you want is some sort of record, then a 35mm compact is your best bet. Modern compacts slip into shirt pockets, and generally weigh under half a pound. They have fixed lenses, usually the moderate wide-angle 35mm, and most are either fully or semi-automatic. The big advantage is that being fairly small and unobtrusive, they're ideal for candid shots, and their simplicity makes them just right for quick snaps. Most of the fully automatic compacts are virtually idiot-proof. They have automatic exposure and automatic focusing – the film winds on automatically, and even the film speed is set by the camera. All you have to do is point and shoot!

Whilst 35mm film is the most widely available, 110 and disk film cameras offer the same advantages as compacts for pocketable size, and ease of use. The only drawback is that because the film size is smaller, you can't expect the same picture quality you get with 35mm.

More creative photographers will go for a Single Lens Reflex camera, with all the benefits (but extra weight) of extra lenses with different focal lengths. You also have the advantage of seeing the picture exactly as it will appear on film, something which 35mm compacts don't do quite so well. This sort of camera is much better if you're contemplating action photography, or wildlife. Lightweight travellers have to consider carefully the benefits of a flexible camera system, against the extra weight penalty. An SLR body with a short range zoom, something like 28 or 35 to 80mm is a good compromise. Some purists argue that a zoom lens never delivers the same quality that you get from a fixed focal length lens. I suppose if you're doing laboratory tests on the things, it's probably true. But zoom lenses are so good these days, there isn't any noticeable lack of quality, even when you start enlarging pictures, where you'd most expect to see any distortion or lack of sharpness.

Apart from the availability of your type of film, do make sure your camera has fresh batteries when you set off, and if possible, have a spare set, just in case something goes wrong. Other useful items to carry, even for the non-dedicated holiday snapper, are a small blower brush for cleaning dust out of the camera when changing film, and some lens cleaning tissues or a specially impregnated cloth.

It's quite easy for photographers to weigh themselves down with all sorts of gear and accessories, and it's quite likely they'll return from a trip to find they didn't use half of it. In fact, I reckon that there's a direct relationship between the amount of gear you carry, and what you actually use. The more you carry, the less you use!

But for some really useful accessories to pop into a gadget bag, consider the following: Polarising filter, used to reduce unwanted glare. A graduated grey filter, used to put a bit of life into washed out skies. Best to get one of the system type filters like Cokin rather than the screw in version. The reason for this is that the position of the line where the graduation from clear to grey takes place alters depending on the aperture you select on the lens. With the filter either sliding in its holder, or just held in front of the lens (as I do), you can use your aperture preview (stop down) button, and then move the filter to give the desired effect.

'Don't be alarmed — my foolproof, fully automatic pocket tripod has gone off in my pocket!'

A pocket tripod can be quite useful, either for setting the camera up to do self portraits using the delayed action shutter release, or for doing time exposures, where the camera needs to be free from shakes.

If you're carrying anything more than a pocket sized camera, you should have some decent carrying equipment. Aluminium cases look very flashy, but they're totally unsuitable for the fast-moving, travelling photographer. Who wants to lug a bulky thing like that about, and then have to plonk it on the ground and open it up to sort out what you need for a particular shot? And the smart shiny leather gadget bags made by the individual camera manufacturers look far too flashy. If it has Nikon, Pentax, Canon or Olympus emblazoned on the outside as well, it's just asking to be stolen.

The best means of carrying gear is one of the many soft camera bags. The better ones incorporate closed cell foam padding which protect camera gear not just from knocks and bumps, but from sudden changes in temperature as well. For the more active, there are also individual camera and lens pouches, made to attach either to a separate belt, or to rucksack belt or harness.

CAMP SITES

My own preference when sleeping 'under canvas' is to camp wild. But often it's not practical to do so, and indeed, in countries like Holland, it's also illegal. Whilst you may have to pay for your pitch, you can at least be certain that you'll have facilities such as a shop either on site, or very close nearby. And a hot shower may be just the thing after a long day's travelling.

The standard of camp sites varies enormously, from the small farm type site with minimal facilities, to the massive international sites, with swimming pools, barbecues, club rooms and supermarkets. For camping in the UK, you can do no better than by becoming a member of the Camping and Caravanning Club. Their site handbook is about as comprehensive as you can get, listing camp sites, and detailing their facilities. For camping abroad, you'll probably be able to get details on some of the larger sites from the appropriate national tourist office. Other than that, finding those idyllic little sites tucked away off the beaten track, well, it's down to you to get out there and discover them!

Some countries require you to have a Camping Carnet, which verifies your status as a bona-fide camper, and provides evidence of adequate third party insurance. Many foreign camp sites require you to deposit your passport when you check in, which of course adds to the hassle if you need it to exchange money. Most sites will take your carnet instead. Carnets are available through the Camping Club, Cyclists Touring Club, AA and RAC.

CAR HIRE

You might consider renting a car when you arrive at your destination. The two big firms world-wide are Hertz and Avis. Their rates are obviously more than you'd expect to pay at a smaller car hire firm or garage, but on the other hand, they do offer significant advantages. For instance, you can book a car in advance from home very easily, and you're more likely to get exactly the sort of car you want. The big car hire firms have depots near to air and sea ports, and larger railway stations. Many even do courtesy taxi services from airports to depots. The other big advantage with the large firms is that you aren't necessarily confined to a round trip. If you want to do a tour from A to B, you can agree a one-way fee in advance, and drop the car off at your chosen destination without having to worry about returning it to the place from which you picked it up.

CASSETTE PLAYER

Some people swear by them, others swear at them! A small 'Walkman' type cassette player and one or two of your favourite tapes may help alleviate the boredom of a long journey. But exercise a little consideration for your fellow passengers, and keep the volume turned down. Apart from the fact that you might damage your own ears (what?), there's nothing more infuriating than the high-pitched rattle which everyone else has to endure. Interesting but true facts number 398: Everyone on a train with a Walkman always seems to be listening to Dire Straits!

Dedicated listeners should have a spare set of batteries standing by for emergencies. A small cassette recorder can add an extra dimension to your travels by capturing some of the evocative sounds. Try some of these: the busy hubbub of souks, bazaars and street markets; ceremonies and festivals; even animals (the cavernous gurglings of a camel are terrific!) You can even use your cassette recorder more imaginatively by using it as an audio diary, recording some of your thoughts and impressions, and capturing some background atmosphere as well. Try it on a train, out in the market, or beside a stream.

Don't expect fantastic results if your machine only has a built-in microphone, as it will tend to pick up some noise from the motor, and any movement whilst being handled. Good fun, though.

CHECK-IN – *See also Baggage*

Arrive in plenty of time to check in for flights or sailings. The same is true if you're doing a long bus or rail journey, simply because you can give yourself the best chance of a good seat. If you haven't any baggage to check in, you can usually cut things much finer. But don't leave it till the last minute. Many airlines overbook seats, particularly on routes with frequent business travellers, because there is usually a certain percentage of last-minute cancellations. The reason for this is that business travellers book seats on several flights to ensure they get one at the time they want, and then cancel the rest at the last moment. In order to avoid making a loss on such cancellations, airlines often overbook seats on flights by up to 25%. So if you haven't got your seat allocation and the flight is full, you may find yourself catching a later flight. Passengers who are 'bumped' in this way are entitled to free hotel accommodation and meals in the event of any significant delay.

It's whilst getting your seat number that you have the chance to say what sort of seat you want. Most airlines give you the choice of smoking or no smoking seats. Personally, I don't think there should be a choice. All seats should be **NO** smoking. Some airlines appear awfully considerate when they tell you that 'for the convenience of passengers, smoking cigars and pipes is not allowed.' Who are they kidding? The imaginary line between smoking and no smoking seats doesn't seem to stop the foul stuff from drifting all over the cabin. I was once allocated a 'No Smoking' seat which was flanked on all sides by 'Smoking' seats. Work that one out if you can!

But apart from reading the clean air act, you may also get the chance to say whether you want a window or aisle seat. On short flights, you may prefer to get a window seat if you can, especially if the views are likely to be good. On long haul flights, the long legged might opt for an aisle seat, where you can stretch your legs, and play at tripping up the hostesses. It also puts you in a good position for getting up for a wander, or to pay those necessary little visits. The only drawback is that you're likely to be just nodding off to sleep when the passenger in the next seat decides to clamber over you in order to go and pay his little visit!

CHILDREN

Your biggest enemy when travelling with children is **BOREDOM**! Children are much like adults, but they don't appreciate superb views or 'interesting' villages. Depending on how light you're travelling, you can keep them amused with books or games. But the best remedy for a bored child is a Walkman cassette player and some children's story cassettes. It staves off boredom simply because there's no effort involved to listen.

For everyone to get the best out of their trip, parents and offspring, you need to do your homework.

CHOLERA

Plan your sightseeing around points of interest, and read up about them the night before you arrive. If not, have the guide books to hand, and make sure you use them. In this way, you can tell your flock a little bit about the background to the area or city, its history and people. Don't just preach from the book, though. Embellish it with your own feelings or opinions (children don't have our experiences and memories to draw upon).

Children can travel in a bubble where the world is only a moving picture. Make the places real, and they can take an interest. It adds to their understanding of the world, and helps make their experiences more memorable.

CHOLERA

Cholera is an acute form of diarrhoea, spread in countries where sanitation is poor, and usually occurs in epidemics. Vaccination for visits to affected areas is no longer mandatory, although it is obviously advisable. Cover from the injection lasts approximately six months, and whilst not totally effective, is better than nothing.

CLIMATE — *See also Clothing, appendix for world-wide temperatures*

Part of your advance planning should include some thoughts as to what sort of weather you're likely to encounter, so you can dress accordingly. The various sections on clothing, along with the sample clothing lists at the back of the book should give you a good idea what to take along.

But it isn't just a question of clothing. If you have to travel at a certain time of year, so be it. On the other hand, a bit of homework will establish what seasons are likely to be more comfortable. If you're interested in wild flowers, a visit to a very hot country will probably pay more rewards in the springtime, rather than mid-summer, when everything has been burnt to a frazzle. And the Asian countries are best avoided during the monsoon seasons unless you have an affinity with ducks.

CLOTHING — *See also T-Shirts, Trousers, Waterproofs, Warmwear, Underwear, Socks, Hat, Gloves*

The key (or at least one of the keys) to lightweight travelling is good comfortable clothes.

Since most modern means of travel involve hours on end of sitting down, you don't particularly want to wear anything constricting that'll leave you feeling as though you've been shrink-wrapped. And if you're travelling from one climate to another, with 'tinned' micro-climates in between varying from hot and fetid to downright chilly, the best approach to clothing is a number of light layers which can be removed or added to as required.

It may appear superfluous to point out that without care, your clothing can cause either offence or get you into trouble in some parts of the world. Take the recent vogue for walkers and backpackers for wearing military style clothing. We even had military DPM (Disruptive Pattern Material) Gore-Tex generally available at one point a few years back. Presumably the people wearing it enjoyed pretending to be Rambo, but I heard of one instance of a climber attired in para-military style in the Pyrenees being shot at!

There are plenty of other places where such garb will attract at the very least the unwelcome attentions of the authorities, and at worst, a bullet. You also need to be aware that not everyone appreciates your walking around in bare arms and legs. Temples and churches may require you to cover up, head included. So swot up on some of the local conventions, and dress for the occasion.

Individual items are covered in more detail under their separate headings, and it goes without saying that travel clothes such as those made by Rohan are ideal, not just because they're extremely comfortable in use, but because you can wash and dry them in a matter of hours. Some of my Rohan gear has been used for wilderness walking from the Scottish Highlands to the Himalayas, and after a quick wash, has been more than presentable to wear in posh restaurants. That's what I call versatile!

COMMUNICATIONS – *See also Telephoning Home*

One of the biggest joys of travelling is to leave behind such things as people who want to pester you, but I accept that not everyone wants to remain out of touch when they're abroad. If you aren't sure of your precise address before you go, people can always write to you Poste Restante. Letters will be held for you at the post office, and will be handed over on production of suitable identification. A passport is the obvious choice. Make sure that potential correspondents address their envelopes clearly, preferably leaving out titles (Mr, Mrs, Ms, Dr, etc.), and putting your surname first. It might sound weird, but bear in mind that

---

otherwise, someone might just file my letter in the
pigeon-hole for 'C' for Clive rather than 'T' for Tully.
Just as likely is the possibility of it going in 'M' for Mr.,
or 'F' for FRGS.

If you use any American Express services, either
holding a charge card, or you have some of their
traveller's cheques, you're entitled to have mail
directed to one of their offices abroad.

COMPASS

If you're navigating your way across unfamiliar
terrain, particularly in wild country, you should have a
compass, and you ought to be able to use it in
conjunction with a map. A small pocket compass from
the Silva range should suit most walkers and off road
cyclists.

A typical model has a transparent plastic base
plate, so as not to obscure any detail when placed on a
map, and the compass housing is liquid filled to
dampen movement of the needle. A calibrated dial can
be rotated on the top of the compass, which, like a
protractor, is calibrated in degrees. (Not always —
some military compasses are calibrated in mils, where
the scale is divided into 6400 graduations. Not much
use to the average traveller unless he's contemplating
whistling up an air strike.)

By taking a bearing from two easily identifiable
landmarks which can be plotted on the map, it's
possible to establish your precise position. All you do is
point the direction of travel arrow on the compass at
the object on which you're sighting, and rotate the 360
degree mark round to where the compass needle is
pointing (which is north). Note however that the
compass needle points to magnetic north, which
actually varies from true north. So when reading the
number of degrees from the index line of the compass,
you should then adjust it for the local variation, which
is generally marked on the map.

At this point, you align the orienteering arrow
and lines on the compass with the north/south grid
lines on the map, and with one side of the compass
base plate lined up with the feature on which you're
sighting, with the direction of travel arrow pointing
towards the feature. Draw a line on the map through
the feature back towards your position, go through the
same procedure with another feature, and the point
where the lines cross is your position on the map. You
merely have to reverse the actions in order to take, say,
the line of a footpath on the map, and transfer the
bearing to your compass. Then, providing you walk
with the orienteering lines of the compass parallel with
the needle (which is pointing to magnetic north, of

course), the direction of travel pointer will keep you on track. Simple, really.

CONDOMS

AIDS isn't the only risk open to the travelling sexual adventurer. There are, of course, a wide variety of other unpleasant diseases which can be contracted by sexual contact. Condoms help reduce the risk, and are a cheap form of insurance. So, ladies and gents, if there's a chance of any such encounters, keep a packet in your pocket or purse.

A condom can make a useful item of equipment to handle a variety of emergencies. It has a fair capacity for water provided it's reinforced with something like a box, or a stronger bag.

CONSTIPATION

Quite a common occurrence amongst travellers, especially when a change in diet, time zones and climate is involved. Left to its own devices, your body usually settles down within two or three days — in fact, worrying about it seems to prolong it. Eat plenty of fruit and vegetables (fibre), and drink lots. If it comes to it, a gentle acting laxative such as the one provided in Rohan's Travelaid should do the trick.

CONTACT LENSES

You may like the look of yourself better with contact lenses rather than glasses, but the little devils can be a bit of a pain when it comes to travelling. I remember the sad but amusing sight of a group in Iceland all going down on hands and knees in a remote valley, to try and find some poor unfortunate's fallen lens. Contact lenses also prove impractical where there's a lot of dust in the air, as they cause considerable irritation, and keeping them clean can be an added problem.

CONTRACEPTIVES

If you're taking the contraceptive pill, make sure your supply is adequate to see you through your trip. Fresh supplies may not be so easily available abroad. In fact, it's better to work on the assumption that they're impossible to get hold of. When crossing time zones, your sleeping pattern becomes altered, and it's easy to allow yourself to go more than 24 hours without taking a pill. Make the adjustment go the other way, so the time between doses is less, rather than more, than a day. Bear in mind too that if you get a touch of diarrhoea, the pill may not be absorbed, so take care!

CONVERTIBLE TRAVEL BAG

A rucksack is by far the most efficient means of carrying your luggage — much better on your back than giving you extra-long arms! In fact, I can't remember the last time I used a suitcase. As I step off the train at airport or harbour, I always smile at the inevitable scramble of two hundred people fighting to be first to grab one of the dozen or so luggage trolleys scattered along the platform. Me, I just shoulder my rucksack and stride past! But rucksacks can be a problem for the international traveller, in more ways than one.

First and foremost, they have rather a lot of straps and other odd bits and pieces hanging all over the place, and very tasty morsels they must be for the conveyor belts and luggage carousels. They also tend to be irregular shapes, and easily jam in the aforementioned machines, sometimes with disastrous effects. It wouldn't be so bad if the baggage handlers spent an extra second placing your sack squarely in the middle of the conveyor. But no, luggage is tossed from trolley to conveyor one after the other without pause. And whilst flat-sided, hard and smooth items of luggage can take this sort of treatment, it only needs one strap to slip down the wrong crack, or for your rucksack to be half hanging over the non-moving edge of the conveyor belt, and the chances are your pack will eventually surface looking like it took one of the supporting roles in the 'Texas Chain-saw Massacre'.

Consider also how it's likely to be thrown into the baggage hold of an airliner, and you can bet your bottom traveller's cheque that your rucksack will be under about five tons of luggage, with one or two straps wrenched off where the handler made it 'fit' into a gap that some other suitcase wouldn't. Sounds horrifying, doesn't it? And whilst this sort of thing obviously doesn't happen to all rucksacks, I have seen several instances where such luggage has been damaged in transit. The cheap rucksacks are usually the least able to take such abuse. Poor materials, poor manufacture, if anything is likely to show them up, it's a trip on an aeroplane.

Travel bags which convert to rucksacks, or rucksacks which convert to travel bags, aren't a terribly new idea, but they're certainly pretty popular these days. The idea, basically, is an internal frame rucksack, with the harness concealed when not in use by zipping a panel over it. In this way, all the major straps likely to cause a jam are out of harm's way, and a well designed convertible will no longer look like a rucksack, more like a smart piece of soft luggage.

Apart from anything else, it's a tremendous help not to have the stigma of a rucksack when travelling in some countries. You don't have to go far in the world to discover that travellers with rucksacks are accorded more attention than those with an anonymous suitcase. If you're carrying a rucksack, the chances are you're on drugs! There's also a reasonable possibility that even if you can afford a hotel room, they suddenly decide they're full up when they see you march in with a pack on your back. Not fair, is it?

The answer has been to combine modern rucksack technology with designs more compatible with international travel, so you get all the benefits of a rucksack, and none of the disadvantages. Berghaus and Karrimor both make excellent convertible bags, offering established adjustable harness systems. They have a fairly comprehensive set of compression straps to take up any free play in the bag, and these double as accessory straps for side pockets. If you were using one of the bags for foreign backpacking, the best way would be to carry your side pockets as cabin luggage in a plastic bag, and mount them up once you arrive at the point where you start walking.

The last main thing to consider with travel bags is security. It's a sad fact that wandering hands can take advantage of the fact that you're not standing over your bag, and soft luggage secured by nothing more than a zip is particularly susceptible. You can at least make it difficult for the little blighters. The bags I've described have two-way zips with pullers which can be locked together. Mind you, a small padlock can be sprung open by a screwdriver with consummate ease, so in high-risk areas, you could neatly wind some wire through the zippers as well. The only drawback comes as you whiz through the 'Nothing to Declare' corridor, and a voice politely and firmly invites you to reveal what you're carrying!

CREDIT CARDS – *See also Money*

Credit cards are an increasingly useful way of making purchases abroad, indeed, in America, they almost treat you like a leper if you haven't got a charge or credit card. What, cash? Access, part of the world-wide Master Card system, and Visa, and for the more affluent, charge cards such as Diners Club and American Express, are all accepted in a good number of the larger shops, particularly in the tourist areas. You'll almost certainly be able to use them to make your purchases in most Duty Free Shops.

CREDIT CARDS

Vouchers for purchases abroad generally take longer to appear on your statements, and provided the pound is strong against the local currency, you could come out of the deal better than you thought. The reason is that the exchange rate which applies to the transaction is the one in force at the time the voucher arrives at the issuing bank, rather than the day on which the purchase was made. Of course, it can also work against you if the pound is weak against the local currency.

A credit card also gives you the means to extra cash when you need it, as you can use it for advances from a bank, and to buy foreign currency or travellers cheques. Note that credit card companies charge interest from the day of the advance, unlike any other purchases, where interest is charged from the date of the monthly statement on which your purchase appears. There's also a handling charge of 1½% which is added to the amount of your advance. But for normal purchases, there's no extra charge at the point of sale — at least there shouldn't be. If anyone tries loading a price because 'they have to pay commission to the credit card company', refuse to buy, and report them to the appropriate credit card company.

In Britain, the Consumer Credit Act gives you the right to involve the credit card company with any purchase where the goods prove to be faulty, or services paid for don't come up to scratch. For travellers, it's ideal. Not only does booking your holiday and travel tickets with a credit card give you a modicum of personal accident cover, it means you haven't chucked your money down the drain if the travel company happens to get there first.

Like anything else, you should have a separate note of your credit card numbers, plus the 24 hour telephone numbers, in case you lose them. Credit card companies absolve you from all but the first £50 of any criminal's spending spree with your cards, provided the loss is reported to them by telephone immediately, and confirmed in writing within seven days.

If you have several cards, it can make life a lot simpler to pay the nominal annual charge to register your cards and other valuable documents with one of the credit card protection firms. They keep a computer log of all the numbers, and in the event of your losing them, one reverse charge (collect) call to them will set the wheels in motion for cancelling the cards and issuing you with new ones. Schemes like the one offered by Card Protection Plan also arrange an instant cash advance and airline tickets, so a loss won't leave you stranded.

DEATH

Like any other aspect of life, travel has its casualties, whether by accident, illness, or just by turning up your toes after your designated innings. By taking out travel insurance, you not only cover yourself from all the misfortunes which travelling can heap upon you, you also take away the distress which your relatives would suffer having to finance the disposal of your body when you've keeled over in some distant land.

There's a story which a friend of mine in the travel trade told me, and which he suggests is almost legendary in the business. It concerns a chap who'd been saving to make a journey of a lifetime to Australia. A flight out to Aus is a long haul, and the gentleman made the most of the constant attention paid by the hostesses, and he tucked into the in-flight meals and drinks with relish. Then, on the last leg of the journey, something terribly inconvenient befell him. He died. Perhaps the excitement was too much for him — sad to think he was within two hours of touching down onto his 'promised land' when he opted for the permanent out of body experience.

On arrival in Australia, the British Consul was contacted, who made efforts to find some next of kin in England. It transpired that the only relative was the man's sister.

'If he wants to blow his life savings on some silly jaunt, and not take out any insurance, don't expect me to bail him out', exclaimed the sister.

'But he's dead', pleaded the official.

'No, we haven't seen him for years. Do what you like with him, we don't want to know!' The perplexing message flashed across to the other side of the world, leaving the Australian authorities still wondering what to do. Then some bright spark came up with the answer.

The deceased received a pauper's cremation. To save further public expense, the airline, who still had his luggage, claimed the urn containing his ashes, and packed it inside. And so it was that our traveller returned to England, packed in his own suitcase, travelling as unaccompanied baggage!

DELAYS — *See also Attitude*

It's inevitable that at some time in your travels, you're going to be subject to delays. If you're travelling by bus or train, with an airline departure or ship sailing at the end of the journey, it pays to allow extra time whenever possible, just to cover the possibility of the unexpected.

DIARRHOEA

Easy to say that, of course, but it can be pretty frustrating to bust a gut getting to the airport on time, to find the departure has been delayed. Spending several hours waiting in a stiflingly hot airport terminal is enough to test anyone's patience. Airlines should make provision for supplying refreshments if the delay is more than an hour or so, and if it involves an unplanned stay overnight, they should also provide hotel accommodation, or put you on another flight.

You also have to accept that other people may take life at a slower pace — infuriatingly so when you really are in a hurry. But take care, because excessive cajoling may just make the wheels turn slower still!

DIARRHOEA

Call it Delhi Belly, Kathmandu Quickstep, Gippy Tummy, Montezuma's Revenge, the Trots, or one of any number of names from a list as long as a roll of toilet paper. You don't need to have taken a slug of the local water to cause an upset. Quite often it's just a change in routine and diet. It can be deucedly inconvenient, not to mention embarrassing, but the best thing is to let nature take its course. You probably won't feel like eating anyway, but do keep up a good intake of fluids. Diarrhoea has a dehydrating effect. Clean, sterilised water with some glucose and salt should help the condition clear up on its own. If it persists after three days, you may have to resort to medication, or seek the advice of a doctor.

There's no fool-proof method of preventing a tummy upset, but a few simple precautions can go a long way towards helping. Like washing your hands thoroughly before eating or preparing food. If you suspect your water supply, boil it, or use purification tablets. In hot countries, be especially wary when you go out to eat in restaurants. Ask if you can inspect their kitchen, and see the food being prepared before you commit yourself to anything. Be wary of what you eat, avoiding any raw meat or fish, and any food which might have been left standing, and then re-heated.

DIARY

Even on short journeys, it pays to keep some sort of diary. It doesn't matter if it's nothing more than a few scribbled cryptic notes, jotted down just before you go to bed. It'll make your journey that much more memorable, and keep you sane once you're back in that humdrum existence you long to escape from again. It's also pretty useful when it comes to straining the memory for names to put to those photographs. It may not have seemed worth while noting what it was you photographed at the time, but you'll wish you had when you get your photos developed a month later.

Once you get into the habit of keeping a travel diary, you might try being a little more creative with it. Don't just note down places visited. What about all those interesting people you've met? Conversations, ideas, or more practical things like recipes for local dishes. Travelling would be a bit sterile without your coming across one or two characters, so remember them when you have your pen and paper to hand!

DISEASES — *Where, how, and how not to get them* — *See also individual entries*

AIDS
Area prevalent: World-wide, but particularly in Europe, North and South America, and Central Africa.
Caught by: Having sex with an infected person, or from injections with infected blood or needles.
Prevented by: No vaccination available, and no cure if full disease develops. Use of condom gives some protection.

Cholera
Area prevalent: Africa, Asia, Middle East, especially where poor hygiene and sanitation exists.
Caught by: Consuming contaminated food or water.
Prevented by: Vaccination by injection, valid for six months. Not totally foolproof, so care should be taken over food and drink.

DISEASES

Infective Hepatitis
Area prevalent: Most parts of the world where poor hygiene and sanitation exists.
Caught by: Consuming contaminated food or water, or by contact with an infected person.
Prevented by: Vaccination available. Care should still be taken over food and drink.

Malaria
Area prevalent: Africa, Asia, Central and South America.
Caught by: Bite from infected mosquito.
Prevented by: No vaccination available. Anti-malarial tablets should be taken for duration of visit to affected area, and for prescribed period before and after visit. Avoid being bitten by covering arms and legs after sunset, using mosquito nets and by using insect repellents.

Polio
Area prevalent: World-wide except Australia, New Zealand, Europe and North America.
Caught by: Direct contact with an infected person. Rarely contracted from contact with contaminated food or water.
Prevented by: Vaccination available. Still best to take care over food and drink.

Rabies
Area prevalent: Many parts of the world.
Caught by: Bite, scratch or lick from infected animal, mainly dogs, cats, foxes, bats and monkeys, but could be others. Always fatal once symptoms develop.
Prevented by: Vaccination recently available, but it only extends the safe period to get to hospital. Valid for three years. Always seek immediate medical attention if bitten.

Tetanus
Area prevalent: Places where medical facilities are not readily available.
Caught by: Infection of open wounds.
Prevented by: Vaccination available. Wounds should always be cleaned thoroughly.

Tuberculosis
Area prevalent: Asia, Africa, Central and South America.
Caught by: Airborne from infectious persons.
Prevented by: Vaccination available.

Typhoid
Area prevalent: World-wide except Australia, New Zealand, Europe and North America, where poor hygiene and sanitation exists.
Caught by: Taking contaminated food, water or milk.
Prevented by: Vaccination available, valid three years.

Yellow Fever
Area prevalent: Africa and South America.
Caught by: Bite from infected mosquito.

Prevented by: Vaccination available, valid ten years. Also take same precautions as with malaria to avoid being bitten.

DRIVING

For the first timer, driving abroad can seem rather daunting, and not a little complicated. But it only takes ten minutes or so to start getting the feel of driving on the 'wrong' side of the road. It can help if you plan your journey so as not to coincide with rush hour traffic in the larger towns. Bear in mind too that rush hours can happen either side of lunch-time, as well as mornings and evenings.

There are greater demands on your concentration, of course. The likely times when you might forget you're supposed to drive on the right are when turning onto an empty road, especially if you're turning left. Roundabouts are a favourite distraction. Try going anti-clockwise! The fact that (assuming you're driving a right-hand drive vehicle) you're sitting in the near side seat means that you need to take extra care when overtaking. A front seat passenger can help here. You should be certain you have plenty of clear distance to overtake before pulling out.

Long distance driving is very good at bringing all your car's faults to light. Have the old banger serviced before setting off on a foreign excursion, and make sure you stock up with an adequate supply of spares. A distributor cap for a Maseratti might be in somewhat short supply in Bulgaria.

Always keep your petrol tank full when long-distance driving, particularly if you're travelling at night. You never know how far it might be to the next petrol station. And unlike in Britain, many foreign service stations don't accept credit cards. In Italy, some don't even accept Eurocheques! So the rule of thumb has to be keep plenty of cash with you, and if you spot a credit card garage, use it.

Essential items to check before setting off are as follows: Brakes and tyres — an obvious number one for safety, particularly if you're motoring over Alpine passes. Don't forget to check the spare tyre.
Exhaust system — Don't bank on finding any 'free-fit' or even 'fast-fit' exhaust services on the continent. A packet of exhaust bandage and repair paste can make temporary repairs on any parts that start to blow.
Radiator hoses — always more likely to go on long journeys, particularly where overheating is likely to be a problem.
Carburettor, plugs and points — all items which can contribute to poor running and excessive fuel consumption.

DRUGS

Lights and indicators – don't forget headlight deflectors.
Wing mirrors – makes overtaking a little easier.

The motoring organisations hire out spares kits for many popular makes of car, on a sale or return basis. The basics they include are: spark plugs, contact breaker points, fan belt, condenser, rotor arm, head gasket set, top and bottom radiator hoses, by-pass hose, electrical fuses. You can just as easily make up your own kit, of course, and you might consider adding these extras: ignition coil, distributor cap, HT leads, alternator brushes, starter motor brushes, windscreen wiper blades, clutch cable, fuel pump repair kit.

Most motorists have some form of tool kit, but there are a few other items which ought to be included, some of which are compulsory:
Breakdown triangle – Compulsory. Make sure you get one which complies with EEC regulations.
Beam deflectors.
Spare set of bulbs – Compulsory in many countries.
Fire extinguisher.
Spare set of keys.
First Aid Kit.
Emergency windscreen.
Radiator sealing compound.
Tool kit – A plug spanner, a few screwdrivers and an adjustable wrench make a bare minimum. Better to have proper spanners or small socket set covering the most often used sizes of nuts and bolts.

DRUGS

It goes without saying that anyone with the intelligence to read this book shouldn't be anyone who either takes drugs, or who would consider carrying them across frontiers for someone else. Prisons in the UK may not exactly be pleasant places to while away a few years, but compared with others, they're positively luxurious! And don't forget that there are countries where the penalty for drug trafficking is not just a long stretch inside, but a long stretch at the end of a rope! Pleading that you're British, or of abnormally low intelligence, doesn't give you a better chance either, as proved in the recent case where the Malaysians hanged a Brit for drug trafficking.

It may sound obvious, but whatever you do, don't accept packages from people 'to help him carry his luggage'. People have been caught out more than once by that trick. It's even worth checking your luggage where someone could conceivably slip something in it without your knowledge. Report any approaches to the nearest security person you can find.

DUTY FREE

Duty free prices vary from one place to another, and it's quite possible that some purchases may not be the bargains you'd think they ought to be. For example, on the non-consumable side, such things as photographic and hi-fi equipment in the duty free shop at Heathrow can actually be bought in many UK retail shops for considerably less. Alcohol and cigarette prices tend to be keener, although I suspect that most places will have to go a long way to compete with the £3.50 I paid for a litre of Glenfiddich at the duty free shop in Dubai!

You are allowed to bring a certain amount of goods back into the country without paying any duty. This duty free allowance varies, depending on whether you've travelled from an EEC country, or elsewhere. The current allowances are as follows:

	EEC	Elsewhere
Tobacco goods		
Cigarettes	300	200
or cigarillos	150	100
or cigars	75	50
or tobacco	400 grams	250 grams
Alcoholic drinks		
Over 38.8° proof	1½ litres	1 litre
or not over 38.8° proof	3 litres	2 litres
or fortified/sparkling wine	3 litres	2 litres
and still table wine	5 litres	2 litres
Perfume	90 ml	60 ml
Toilet water	375 ml	250 ml
Other goods	£250 worth	£32 worth

If your purchases fall within these limits, you can walk through the green customs channel — no goods to declare. If you've exceeded these limits, or you aren't sure, then you should walk through the red customs channel — goods to declare.

Note that this is for the UK only. If you intend taking goods into another country, you should pay attention to their own duty free allowances, not all of which seem bounded by the logic of international packaging. India, for example, allows an incongruous .95 litres of spirit, although in practice, they don't seem to bat an eyelid at all the 1 litre bottles that go through. I suspect that it's called into play when they want to be awkward with someone, and, I would imagine they wouldn't be terribly impressed at any efforts by the guilty party to take a swig from his bottle in order to get through!

DYSENTERY

DYSENTERY

Acute diarrhoea, usually containing blood and mucus, accompanied by abdominal pains and fever. Bacillary dysentery is spread by faecally contaminated water, milk or food, or food tainted by flies. Medical treatment is necessary to clear it up.

Amoebic dysentery is a less acute form of the infection, taking at least three weeks to develop. It must still be treated, as if allowed to develop, it can spread to the liver, with much more serious consequences. As with other forms of diarrhoea, it's important to prevent dehydration by taking plenty of water with salt and sugar mixed in.

EAR PLUGS

This isn't as daft as it sounds! If you've ever had to share a room, tent, hostel or railway carriage with someone else, you'll almost certainly have experienced all manner of disturbances, and your sleep will have suffered as a result. Some of my trekking trips have been made quite miserable by having to endure endless choruses of snoring in dormitory accommodation in mountain huts.

The answer is a pair of ear plugs, available from Boots the Chemists in packs of three pairs. They're made from very soft foam which compresses when you roll them between finger and thumb, and they then expand to form a comfortable fit once inserted into each ear. You can also get malleable wax plugs, but they need to be replaced frequently to reduce the possibility of infection. My foam plugs are washable, and they deaden the sound significantly. With the soporific effect from hearing your own heartbeat, I can guarantee you'll get a good night's sleep. My ear plugs have had me snoozing through snoring, cow bells, barking dogs, drums and singing. Don't leave home without 'em!

ELECTRIC CURRENT

Wire we discussing this, you might ask. Indeed, you might wonder watt the point is, but people do need reminding that the electricity supply around the world ain't all the same! Not only does the voltage vary from one country to another, so too does the type of plugs and sockets to get the stuff out of the wall. Some people buy these all-purpose adaptors with sliding pins and bars which will convert a UK three-pin plug to almost anything. It's a bit gimmicky though. If I'm only visiting one country on any one trip, I'd far sooner get the proper plug, and wire it onto the appliance. Better still, get by without, or use battery operated appliances like shavers, and gas curling tongs for the ladies.

On the whole, voltages are either 220/240 volts, or 120. An appliance made to work on 240 volts may still work plugged into 120 volts, but it will only operate at half power. Plug a 120 volt appliance into 240 volts, and invariably there will be a large flash accompanied by lots of smoke. In other words, if your appliance has a voltage selector on it, make sure it's set for the correct one before you plug in.

EMBASSIES and CONSULATES

There are times when the traveller finds himself really thankful that there's generally an embassy or

EMERGENCIES

consulate to hand abroad. The more frequent calls on their services come from travellers who've lost their passports, or who've become the victims of some other misfortune — they may even have been arrested. There are also the occasional problems where a country is experiencing some form of unrest, and British subjects can call if they're worried about the situation.

If you need to make urgent contact, the telegraph address of British embassies throughout the world is **PRODROME**, and all British consulates **BRITAIN**. Note however that they get the best of both worlds when it comes to closing for Bank Holidays, as they observe both British holidays, and those of the host nation.

Whatever your problem, it is the consulate that will help sort things out. It's their job to look after the interests of British nationals abroad, whilst the embassies handle diplomatic affairs between the British Government and the host nation. You generally find them at the same address, but not always. If you happen to find yourself in dire straits in a country without a consulate, your best bet is to look for one belonging to a friendly nation — a Commonwealth country with some clout, like Canada or Australia, or a neutral like Switzerland or Sweden. They should at least point you in the right direction.

Some people have the mistaken idea that consulates can cure all problems. They can issue emergency passports, and give advice on how you can get funds transferred to you. They might even cash a cheque for you. But don't expect them to bail you out if you can't pay medical bills, or for them to interfere in local judicial procedures if you've been arrested. If you find yourself financially embarrassed, they can, as a last resort, repatriate you to the UK, although the expense of doing so is merely a loan which you're expected to repay promptly once you're home.

EMERGENCIES

If you get into really desperate problems abroad, then you should contact the nearest British Consulate. Typical problems might be your being arrested, or having your passport, or all your belongings stolen. Any problems with local authorities can often be smoothed over by approaching the Consulate.

If you happen to be in a situation far from help, up in the hills, desert or jungle, you ought to have considered all the possibilities already. Your survival depends on your being able to weigh up the problems calmly. Is your situation life- threatening? Can you move somewhere safer? What are your supplies like? You can last for a considerable period without food, but your chances diminish significantly if you can't get water. Will anyone miss you, and set a search in motion when you don't turn up? If someone is likely to search for you, it's usually better to stay where you are, and make yourself comfortable.

Injuries and illness also have to be considered. A party might have to split, leaving some to look after anyone unable to move, whilst others go to fetch help. First and foremost, protect yourself against a hostile environment, and the possibility of being exposed to further dangers — falling rocks, avalanches, bad weather. Assuming your navigation is up to scratch, you should know where you are, and can then make a decision on the viability of trying to go for help, or sitting it out.

Ultimately, it pays to have the muscle of good insurance behind you. Travellers to the wild places in the UK enjoy the privilege of being rescued by the volunteers of the mountain rescue teams. And provided your predicament wasn't brought about by sheer stupidity in the face of sensible advice, you won't get a bill for calling out the RAF's Search and Rescue helicopters — it goes down as training flights. Elsewhere, you have to pay to be rescued, and it isn't cheap. Climbers can expect to pay something like £7 **per minute** for professional rescue services in the French Alps, and even more in Switzerland! Moral of the story? Insure yourself to the hilt. Standard travel insurance won't cover you for technical climbing, but the British Mountaineering Council can help out here.

FILM

FILM – *See also Camera, Photography, X-Ray*

If you travel with a camera, you'd be well advised to lay in plenty of supplies of film. In fact, it's best to take more than you think you'll need. In many countries, film is very expensive, even the most common 35mm films. You could find yourself paying up to three or four times what you would at home. The other factor is that you can't be too sure on the quality of the film stock, particularly if you buy in hot countries, and where the retailer hasn't considered the possibility of refrigerating his film in order to keep it in prime condition, or where the film could simply be substantially out of date.

It isn't even very prudent to leave buying your film until you get into any duty free shops. Their prices are generally higher than what you'd find buying from any of the big photographic retailers. The moral of the story is get it all before you go, and make sure you take more than you think you'll need.

The actual type of film you buy obviously depends very much on your type of photography. Colour prints are the most easily viewed when it comes to reliving your travels, but unless the developing and printing comes up to scratch, the results can be disappointing. Cheapo D&P firms run masses of films through their machines all in one go, and the colour and contrast balance may well be set up on someone else's film. If your prints come back with a green, yellow or orange cast, this is the reason. Make sure the printing is done by a firm monitored by Kodak, and you'll be all right.

Colour transparency film can capture much greater depth of colour, but some might find the business of loading slides into a viewer or projector somewhat tedious. Non-process paid films have extra leeway in that you have the possibility of rating them at a different speed from the nominal – useful, because in poor light, you could uprate a 100 ISO film to, say, 400, to give you the extra sensitivity. The developing process has to be altered to suit, of course. Don't do like the chap I bumped into once, and up or down rate your film speed to suit every individual shot!

Main points to remember when it comes to cosseting your film stocks are: don't let anyone X-Ray it. Despite what any notices may say, given sufficient numbers of exposures, X-Rays can and do ruin film. Endeavour to keep it cool, particularly important in hot countries. If you're staying in a hotel, your room may have a refrigerator you can use. Failing that, keep it in your camera bag in the shade whenever possible. The exact opposite in temperature can also have adverse effects on your film. If the temperature drops below freezing, a very likely proposition if you're up in the

mountains, film tends to become very brittle, and can
quite easily become torn if you wind on too
energetically. Keep the camera in its bag until you
actually decide to take a photograph, and prevent it
from becoming exposed to harsh temperatures for too
long.

FIRES

In the normal course of things, I'd recommend a
lightweight camping stove every time for doing the
cooking. It's convenient, safe, provided you use it
sensibly, and it leaves no mark on the environment. In
other countries, where the 'backwoodsman' culture is
practised more earnestly, a blazing fire at your
campsite seems almost de rigueur. Very cosy, but in my
experience, people that build fires don't clear up after
themselves the next morning, leaving a charred patch
of ground to spoil someone else's experience of the
outdoors.

But there could be an emergency situation when
you have to build a fire out of necessity. There are a
number of books on survival which go into the subject
in more detail than I intend to cover here. Briefly, the
key to successful fire lighting is plenty of bone dry
tinder — which could be anything from dried dead
wood to the fuzz which collects in your pockets. If you
have your lighter, all well and good. Failing that, you'll
have to improvise with any one of a number of
ingenious ideas, from using the sun and a magnifying
glass, to a battery shorted out with a piece of wire to
produce sparks.

The important thing for the fire is that it should
be sheltered in order to retain heat for continued
combustion, and to be well ventilated. The most
efficient fire I've seen is an Indian two hole fire, where
the fire is built in a hole in the ground, ventilated by a
tunnel dug through from an adjoining hole. It also has
the advantage that you simply have to fill in the holes
afterwards to cover all trace of the fire.

FIRST AID — *See also Medical Kit*

First aid ranges from minor problems like
dealing with a blister, to full-blown emergencies where
someone has suffered a major injury, and you're the
only person on hand to offer any assistance. Your
medical kit should cope with most of the mundane
problems like cuts and scratches. If you're doing
something a little more adventurous, then you should
have some larger bandages to cope with sprains and
fractures.

But it may be that you'll have to improvise. If the

patient is unconscious, you should remember your ABC of basic life support — that's Airway, Breathing and Circulation. Check first of all that the patient has nothing obstructing the air passage — tongue, dentures, mucus, vomit. If you place your hand under the nape of the neck and lift the head up and back (assuming the patient is lying on his back), you'll put the airway nicely into a straight line, so breathing is easy.

Then look, listen and feel, to check if the patient is actually breathing. If breathing is absent, keep the patient's head tilted back, pinch his nostrils together, take a deep breath, and blow firmly with your mouth sealed tightly over the victim's. Your exhaled air contains more than enough oxygen to keep your patient alive. Give four breaths, checking to see that the patient's chest rises and falls.

Then check for a pulse. Don't mess about trying to feel the wrist. The surest method is to place your hand on the victim's Adam's apple, and then let the fingers slide into the groove in the neck at one side. If there is no pulse, you must try and get the heart beating by cardiac massage. Kneel to one side of the victim, and place one of your hands on top of the other, interlocking the fingers. Place the heel of the lower hand on the lower part of the victim's breastbone (between the nipples), and press straight down 1½ to 2 inches. After 5 compressions, give another breath, and then continue the same pattern, alternating between the two until breathing and circulation return.

You must be prepared to carry on for some considerable time, and if you can alternate with someone else, so much the better. But if you are in remote country, with little or no help, and your patient shows no sign of recovery after three quarters of an hour, as hard as it may be to take, you must accept that your victim is dead. Take advantage of any opportunity to practice resuscitation techniques using St. John's Ambulance manikins. Remember — Airway, Breathing, Circulation.

Once the unconscious victim has a regular pulse, and is breathing normally, roll him over onto his front, and into the recovery position, with the head on one side, and a bent arm and leg brought out at right angles on one side to prevent him accidentally rolling over. The position gives the patient unrestricted breathing, and any vomiting won't choke him.

The last main life support function is to control any major bleeding. Don't tie tourniquets, they're dangerous. Apply pressure directly onto the wound by placing a pad of bandage material to it, and tying a bandage over the top. Don't remove it if blood starts to seep through, but tie more bandage on. The text

books may tell you to heed the requirements of
cleanliness when bandaging a wound, but make sure
you get your priorities right. A person could bleed to
death in the time it might take you to wash your hands,
and find a sterile bandage from your first aid kit. If it's
a gaping wound, stick your fist in it, tear off a piece of
shirt — use anything, but do it quickly!

FOOD — *See also Water, Sanitation*

The prime cause of concern for travellers in areas
where sanitation is less than desirable is to see that all
fruit and vegetables, if to be eaten raw, are thoroughly
washed in clean water. If the water is suspect, it should
be sterilised. Fruits like apples are easiest eaten peeled.
Avoid dairy products, particularly ice cream, and don't
eat undercooked or raw meat. Even in restaurants
purporting to have western standards, beware of re-
heated food.

Vegetarian and vegan travellers have
traditionally been treated with every reaction from
horror to amazement when they've confronted hotels
and restaurants with their life-style. In my experience,
it's usually the large expensive places that seem least
able to cope with 'unusual' requests, and produce
ordinary looking salads, or the standard omelette.

The outlook is promising, though. There's a
much greater awareness of healthy eating, and it's
starting to show, both in restaurants, and in packaged
food. The Vegetarian Society of the UK (see Appendix
for address) produce an excellent guide called the
'International Vegetarian Handbook', which lists the
details of restaurants and hotels catering for
vegetarians and vegans in the UK, and abroad. It also
gives you useful phrases and words in twelve different
languages to get you by in restaurants.

The golden rule when travelling is to let your
travel agent know well in advance what you need.
Airlines usually ask for advance notice of particular
dietary requirements. And it's best to check anyway,
although ferry companies are generally better
equipped to provide vegetarians with a reasonable
choice of food.

FOOD FOR ACTIVE TRAVELLERS

On foot, bicycle, or paddling a canoe, the
lightweight traveller inevitably turns his thoughts to
the question of what food actually helps him perform
more efficiently. The traditional view of hill walkers
stuffing themselves with Mars bars is only part of the
picture. Perhaps the biggest dietary mistake of any

FOOD FOR ACTIVE TRAVELLERS

traveller this century was made by Captain Scott. By all accounts, his team ate well whilst at base camp. But when they set off on their sledges for the South Pole, they took just three basic foods — biscuits, chocolate and butter. Lots of calories for energy, but no vitamin C. The result? The deaths of Scott and his team returning from the Pole were almost certainly due to scurvy.

If you want to prepare yourself for arduous exercise, it simply isn't enough to eat lots. Your body derives energy from various stores, which in turn are kept 'topped up' by your eating. Fat is the most abundant store of energy, even in rakes like me, but the release of energy from fat is relatively slow. When you start exercising hard, your body takes more energy from carbohydrates, stored as glycogen in muscle tissue. These stores are much smaller, hence the reason why strenuous activity quickly leads to exhaustion.

Athletes use a technique called carbohydrate loading, which is just as useful to anyone involved with prolonged strenuous exercise — mountain trekking or hard cycling. Basically, it involves a high carbohydrate diet, but it isn't just a question of shovelling the stuff in. It isn't quite that simple. Several days before you set off, you should exercise to the point of exhaustion. Then, in the following days, exercise mildly, eating your high carbohydrate foods. Normal glycogen levels return within twenty four hours, but then continue to build up. The effect is to delay the onset of fatigue during prolonged exercise.

The following foods are all high in carbohydrate, and low in protein and fat): Breakfast cereals, bread, biscuits, potatoes, rice, pasta, dried fruit, tinned fruit in juice.

Suitable drinks are: Tea and coffee with sugar, Ovaltine, Horlicks, drinking chocolate, lemonade, fruit squashes, fruit juices, moderate amounts of beer or sweet cider.

And these are the ones to avoid: Meat pies, sausage rolls, pastries, large helpings of red meat, hard cheese and cream cheese, oils, butter, margarine, cream and fried foods.

So a day's menu could typically be: **Breakfast:** Porridge / breakfast cereal / pancakes with treacle or syrup. Thick slices of bread with marmalade, jam or honey. Fruit juice.
Main Meal: Thick soup, crusty bread. Small serving of chicken or fish. Large serving of potato, boiled or baked, no added fat. Vegetables. Milk pudding with stewed fruit.
Light Meal: Baked beans on toast **or** any pasta dish with lots of pasta and a small amount of meat sauce or cheese **or** pizza, deep base **or** risotto. Fresh fruit / yoghurt / tinned fruit.

FOOD – LIGHTWEIGHT TRAVELLERS

Snacks: Fruit, energy bars, dried fruit.

There's a fallacy that because the muscles are working hard during exercise you should eat extra protein. The fact is, that once the human body has stopped growing, a man of average weight needs just 53 grams per day. Most people eat at least 100 grams of protein a day, so it isn't necessary to up the intake.

And whilst glycogen loading isn't really appropriate to more casual exercise, the best foods to take are still carbohydrates. Foods high in fat take a long time to digest, and are absorbed slowly, so it's best to avoid them.

FOOD FOR LIGHTWEIGHT TRAVELLERS

Lightweight travellers in remote places need to carry their own food, but the food likely to do the most good also has the most bulk and weight. Removing the water content from food has long been a method used to cut down on these two factors. Apart from improving its ease of transport, it was also found to keep longer, although the essential vitamins and minerals vanished somewhere along the way.

Early attempts in military circles left food tasting bland and unpalatable when rehydrated (I'm told some of it still is!), and preservatives were added to try to make the taste as near as possible to the original. Today, dehydrated foods range from the basic convenience variety, to those specially prepared for backpacking and expeditions, with added vitamins and minerals – and these range from standard fare to the wildly exotic!

Food needs careful planning, especially if you're going on a long trip. Despite the claims of some advertisers, you should realise that there's no substitute for fresh, wholesome, unprocessed, additive-free food. The human body wasn't designed to function on highly processed foods! Having said that, most people accept the convenience factor as a strong reason for using them. Dehydrated is best kept for periods away from civilisation. Supplement your diet with fresh food whenever you can, particularly fruit.

Breakfast: There was a time when I attempted eggs of one sort or another for breakfast. The first idea (and it's still not a bad one!) was to break half a dozen eggs into a wide topped poly-bottle. They keep for two or three days like this, and can be poured out one at a time for cooking. That, at least, was the theory. All too often, I found the whole lot had scrambled itself after a day's march over rough terrain, leaving me with the choice of omelette, scrambled eggs, omelette or omelette for breakfast. Then I tried powdered eggs, but these pasty unnatural dishes bore no resemblance at all to the original thing!

I find a bowl of muesli perfectly adequate to set me in motion, and a big mug of steaming tea washes it down nicely. Assuming you use dried milk, you then have the option of eating your cereal cold, or with hot water on a chilly morning. A certain amount of experimentation will give you an adventurous outlook, but be prepared for failure now and then. I once subjected the editor of 'The Great Outdoors' to the idea of mixing a packet of Kellogg's Rise 'n' Shine into the morning's muesli on a long-distance walk across Scotland. The result was a sickly stodge which left our mouths and tongues bright orange!

Main meal: The choice in dehydrated foods is wide, and determined on your tastes, and the depth of your pockets. Some imported freeze-dried foods from America are very exotic, and you could pay nearly £4 for a single portion. Accelerated Freeze Drying (AFD) is a process which supposedly leaves more flavour in the food, and only requires the addition of hot water to reconstitute it. Mountain House and Raven both make AFD meals, intended for consumption straight from the bags, thus saving wear and tear on your bowl.

Boiling water is poured into the bag of food, stirred, and left for five to ten minutes before eating. The trouble is, you always get a rebellion in the corners of the bag. Despite frantic stirring, you still find some powdery bits at the bottom, and your spoon gets food all the way up the handle. So rule number one for eat-in-the-bag foods is don't. Tip it into your bowl and be civilised! If you insist on eating from the bag, make sure it's standing in a pot when you pour the boiling water in. Those semi-stiff cellophane bags droop all over the place, and become difficult to handle without some support.

You don't have to go to a specialist outdoor shop to get dehydrated foods, of course. Supermarkets and health food shops are useful places to look in. Batchelors make the well-known Vesta range of dried foods, which I've found to be very tasty. Although some of the rice dishes are intended to be made in two separate saucepans, I've noticed no detriment to the old taste buds by slinging the lot into one pan. The calorific content is less than the equivalent portion of, say, a Raven meal, which is formulated specially for active people on the move. The way round this is to use a two-person pack for one, although this tends to be somewhat overwhelming if you're cooking for two.

The other solution is to add something like dried peas and mashed potato to boost the meal. If you add instant mash to stew or vegetable risotto, make sure the main meal is completely rehydrated and ready to serve beforehand. Otherwise, the potato soaks up all the water like a parched sponge, and your meal turns out dry and chewy!

If you prefer to create your own meals, things like noodles, quick rice, dried vegetables, and packet soups are useful. Take a look around the shops, and then experiment at home. Don't tempt providence by venturing out with an untried recipe. Dehydrated foods of the non-instant variety are much more palatable, and require less cooking time, if given the opportunity to soak beforehand. Tip your food into a pot of water before you put the tent up, and it'll be well soaked by the time you're ready to cook.

FOOTCARE

Hopefully, you've already discovered that your feet are an important and integral part of your walking equipment. It doesn't matter how much money you spend on high technology weather-proofs, rucksacks and tents — if you don't actually get out on your tootsies, you might just as well leave your cheque book, charge card or piggy-bank at home. You can, of course, draw a comparison with the old motor tyre advert. Your feet are the only major point of contact with the ground when walking (unless you're drunk), so it makes sense to look after them properly.

General care should go without saying. Keep your feet clean, and the nails well trimmed. Pressure on long toe-nails can end up causing bruising underneath the nail — very painful! If you have any doubts, it would pay you to have a check-up at a chiropodist. Having prepared yourself as best you can, the unspeakable is still likely to happen, so here are a few tips on how to keep going once the great trek has started:

Blisters: I ought to point out that the following remedy is scorned by the medical profession. On the other hand, doctors always work on the premise that you stop doing whatever it is that causes your injury. In this respect, Professor Tully's remedy for blisters is something of a do or die affair. Most medical books will tell you to leave a blister alone, merely covering it up with a plaster. They might also tell you that to stick a needle in it means you run the risk of infection. The point here is that if you intend to carry on walking for more than a day, a blister unlanced will spread, until your foot is in such a state you will have no option but to abort.

The fluid in a blister is actually the body's method of protecting a part which has become chafed, so it's important to ensure that it is adequately protected with a plaster once you have lanced it. Whilst the most likely cause of your blister is feet and boots not having spent enough time together before

FOOTCARE

the great trek, it can also be caused by such things as a small piece of grit in the boot, or even a rucked up sock. If it's possible to remove the cause of the injury, do so.

Lancing the blister is a simple operation, but which should be carried out with care. Place one finger on the blister and exert a slight pressure on it. Then, with a clean tissue at the ready, push your sterilised needle through the skin near the edge of the blister. The fluid will spurt out, but may stop leaking before the whole blister is drained, so this operation may have to be carried out several times before it has gone down. If you do this last thing at night, you can leave it uncovered to get some air to it. It will need further lancing operations over a couple of days before the blister dries out.

You must be sure to sterilise your needle before and after the operation (hold it in the flame of your lighter or stove for a few seconds), and to use a clean tissue every time. Protect the blister with a plaster during the day, lancing it and replacing the plaster with a clean one when you stop for lunch. It's painful going when you start out on a blister, but if you grit your teeth and keep moving, the pain will quickly ease.

As always, prevention is better than cure, and the first sign of a blister forming is a hot spot. Attend to it then with plasters or moleskin, and you could nip it in the bud.

Sprains: If you are unfortunate enough to sprain an ankle, you must accept that you're going to have to stop what you're doing, and report for sick parade. Leave your boot or shoe on, it will help support the injury whilst you have to keep moving. A large bandage tied tightly in a figure of eight around the foot and ankle will give additional support. Once at base, you can take the boot off, and apply cold compresses to limit the swelling.

Footsore?: Walking, trekking, or even just sightseeing can leave the feet feeling tired and achey. I've found that the best thing is a good session of foot massage at the end of the day. Take your socks off (phew!) and rub the soles of your feet with the tips of your fingers, or even finger nails, in small circular motions, and don't be afraid to press quite hard. The feeling is delightful! Knead the feet on both sides, grasping them between fingers and thumbs, and you'll soon find the life coming back into those tired old plates.

You can also get various aerosol foot sprays (all of which cause untold environmental damage!) which contain similar treatments for bacteria, although not so good from the massage point of view. Certainly in hot weather, when your feet perspire a lot, it's best to use something to protect against athlete's foot.

FOOTWEAR — See also Socks, Footcare

Prime rule for travellers is wear something that's comfortable. Don't leave it until you travel to break in a new pair of walking boots, or even new shoes. For a wide variety of applications, you can't beat a good pair of training or running shoes. They have soft uppers, and shock absorbing midsoles — good for walking, travelling or casual wear. Your feet expand when sitting down for long periods of time, because your blood tends to pool in the feet and legs. So you want something which can be removed easily, or at least loosened.

Unless you plan some pretty strenuous mountaineering, you don't need very heavy stiff leather boots for walking. Provided you have support around the ankles, lightweight walking boots will suffice for most levels of trekking. And whilst it's possible to cycle with a pair of trainers, cycle tourers might like to consider a pair of proper cycling shoes, which give an extra bit of stiffness in the sole, and which make pedalling less tiring.

Whatever your footwear, the most important consideration is that boots, shoes or trainers should fit you properly. Don't rush when you're buying. Try on boots or shoes wearing the socks you intend to use with them, and take it from there. It's most important that you allow enough room for the toes, particularly in walking boots. A good rule of thumb (or toe) is to slide the foot forward as far as it can into the unlaced boot. You should now be able to slide a finger down between your heel and the back of the boot. If you can't, try the next size up. Make sure that when the boot is laced up, your heel isn't able to move about. This is prime blister area, so beware!

Leather boots need breaking in, of course, and even the synthetic jobs will feel more comfortable after a period of wear. If you're preparing to go backpacking or trekking with new boots, it's important that you break them in wearing a similar load on your back. Boots that feel comfortable for a casual stroll may feel completely different if you pound away for a day with a loaded rucksack adding to your weight. And don't forget to go for the luxury treatment in socks as well. If you're on your feet much, a pair of loopstitch socks is very comfortable, even in warmer weather.

Insoles are very useful pieces of kit which can ease footsoreness. Cheap foam or felt ones are out — either they don't support the feet adequately, or they give them such a rebound that they chafe in the heel of the boot. Spenco make very good insoles which ensure your feet stay blister-free underfoot, and add a comfortable layer between your feet and the ground. Most lightweight boots now have moulded closed cell

FRACTURES

foam insoles supplied as standard, and they are very good.

Sorbothane is a plastic material capable of absorbing considerable amounts of shock without any rebound. Walking, especially with a pack, sends shocks up the legs and through the spine. Sorbothane pads in the heels reduce impact shock by 50%, so the risk of injury is obviously reduced. Sorbothane is available either incorporated in closed-cell foam footbeds, or as separate heel pads.

FRACTURES – *See also First Aid*

You can tell a cracked or broken bone by pain, swelling and possibly bruising around an injured part. In some injuries, a break is quite obvious if a limb ends up in an abnormal position. If help is likely to come quickly, just do your best to make the patient as comfortable as possible, and prevent him from moving, which could add to the pain and shock.

If you're miles from anywhere, and it's likely to take some considerable time to get medical attention, you'll need to improvise. Once again, the aim is to prevent any further movement at the fracture site. Use tent poles, ski sticks, ice axes or any other material to form a splint, well padded with spare clothing, sleeping mats – anything to make it comfortable. Check regularly that you haven't tied it up too tight and impaired the circulation. You'll notice a change in colour if you have, and the patient may lose some feeling.

You ought to have some decent sized bandages if you're well off the beaten track. A large triangular one will make a sling for a lower arm or hand injury. Failing that, rig up a sling by securing the patient's sleeve to his jacket.

If you're really stuck for splinting material, a broken leg is best treated by using the healthy leg as a splint. Put plenty of padding between the two, and then tie them together. Don't expect your patient to hop!

Once immobilised, and once the patient has recovered from the shock of the accident, a broken bone without any complications shouldn't entail an air evacuation. A patient with a broken arm ought to be able to walk without any trouble – a broken leg case will obviously need assistance.

It's mainly dependent on how much tissue damage occurs, and any subsequent blood loss as to the urgency of getting professional medical help. Quite obviously, if the injury is to the head or spine, you should make the patient comfortable without moving him, set up camp, and then work out a means to summon help as quickly as possible.

GLOVES

I find a thin pair of polypropylene gloves serves most functions in cooler weather. I tend to have my hands in my pockets (unless I'm riding a bike), so the jacket or trousers provide the windproofing. Thin gloves also make it much easier to work cameras. In severe cold, or where there's wind and rain, a pair of fibre-pile mitts work wonders, although they are relatively bulky. Gore-Tex shelled pile mitts are best for mountaineering in winter conditions.

GUIDE BOOKS

It obviously makes sense to do a bit of research on places you're travelling to before you get there, but you can overdo it to the point of taking some of the magic out of a first visit. Basic information about local currency, customs and climate can usually be gleaned from tourist board leaflets. Most tourist offices are very helpful when it comes to answering requests for leaflets and brochures.

But guide books can help shed light on some aspects of a country which a Government backed tourist office would somehow omit to mention — usually the less savoury ones. Nevertheless, you can only prepare yourself so far. If your research produces a detailed itinerary, there's a chance that something along the way may disappoint you. You end up judging a place before you've even arrived there. Gather a few ideas of the things that might interest you. It makes for a more flexible approach, and lets you look at a country with an open mind.

HAT

Two reasons for using a hat. First of all, the massive concentration of blood vessels in your scalp dissipates something like 70% of your total body heat. So when it's cold, it makes sense that the first item of warmwear should be a woolly hat.

When it's very hot and sunny, a brimmed hat like one of those cheap cotton bush hats can perform stirling service by keeping the sun off the back of your neck, and the glare out of your eyes — both of which can give you blinding headaches. But by the same token, do make sure you can get some air to your head when it's really hot. You have more sweat glands per square inch of skin on your scalp than anywhere else, so stay cool!

HEALTH

If in any doubt about your health, get your doctor to give you the once-over. A check-up makes sense if you're going on a long trip, or if you're likely to be involved in anything strenuous, like mountain trekking. For example, high blood pressure, asthma and bronchitis could be a problem at altitude. For longer visits, people with particular health problems who are on specific medications, might consider the possibility of having a doctor's letter outlining their state of health translated into the language of the country they're visiting.

In any event, a small card containing details of your blood group, whether you're diabetic, and have any allergies to drugs, kept in your wallet, could save valuable time in the event of your requiring medical treatment. SOS Talismans are available from jewellers and some department stores, and these small watertight containers fashioned as St. Christopher medals, and worn on chains either around the neck or wrist, contain a slip of paper on which all these details can be recorded, along with names and addresses of next of kin.

If you're planning to travel to exotic places, you might find that even your GP hasn't all the up to date information. MASTA, the Medical Advisory Service for Travellers Abroad (see Appendix for address), has a comprehensive and up to the minute computerised data bank of information on diseases and health hazards throughout the world.

When you order a personalised health brief from MASTA, you tell them what immunisations you've had, and what allergies if any, and what your expected living conditions will be like. From that, they produce a brief of health information, specific to you and the areas you intend to visit for the particular time of year, along with recommended immunisations, and a timetable of when to have them. You can pick up an application form for a health brief from the pharmacist at any branch of Boots the Chemists. There are three different types of brief, from one with the minimum information you would need for your trip, to a comprehensive brief intended more for people working or living abroad.

HEAT EXHAUSTION

The body needs water to maintain temperature control. The way it does it is by the evaporation of sweat to keep you cool. If you don't drink enough, especially in hot conditions, you'll start off feeling extremely thirsty. Then your body temperature starts to rise, you'll feel faint, and eventually you fall into a coma and die. A good rule of thumb is to take 1 pint of water for every 10 degrees Fahrenheit of temperature every 24 hours. In other words, if the temperature's 90, you should be drinking at least nine pints of water every 24 hours.

In fact, when supply isn't a problem, you should always drink more than you need. Don't wait until your mouth feels as though the dog has slept in it! You should also maintain your salt intake, to prevent muscle cramps. Note however that you shouldn't take extra salt without water, as it causes the blood to thicken, and makes your problem even worse.

HEAT-STROKE

Happens when the body's temperature regulating mechanism packs up completely. The skin becomes hot and dry to the touch, and the victim may show some similar symptoms to those of hypothermia, such as unpredictable behaviour and lack of co-ordination. Unless treated, the victim becomes comatose and dies. Cooling is the answer, by fanning, wrapping the patient in wet sheets, or immersing into a cold bath. As with heat exhaustion, avoidance is a lot simpler.

HEPATITIS

Infective hepatitis A is an unpleasant disease of the liver, spread by faecally infected water, and uncooked foods. Hepatitis B, like AIDS, is spread through the use of dirty syringes and casual sexual contact. Both hepatitis A and B are common in India and Pakistan. Gamma globulin provides short-term protection against hepatitis A, and it's generally

---

recommended that you have this injection if you're visiting an affected area. There is a vaccine available for hepatitis B, although it isn't widely available. Not really necessary unless there's a possibility of exposure to the infection.

HI-JACK — *See also Terrorist*

It's one of those things, like an air crash, or being burgled, that the majority would tend to put at the back of their minds. But it's worth considering. What **would** you do if terrorists with guns and grenades suddenly took control of your aircraft, and used you as a hostage? It's an unfortunate fact of life that the various quarters of political extremism look upon hi-jacks as a justifiable means to publicise their cause, or to extract some form of ransom.

The typical scenario is one where the airliner ends up sitting on the tarmac of some airport, with gunmen making demands, and threatening the lives of the aircraft's passengers. Your life! It usually works out that the terrorists try to single out one or two people of whom they can make an example — and nine times out of ten, anyone with an American passport comes top of the list, with Brits not far behind.

People who've found themselves in these dangerous situations recommend that the best course of action is not to draw attention to yourself. The ones that start arguing or preaching to the man with the gun are generally the ones to get the bullet first.

Don't look them in the face, speak only when spoken to, and sit as low in your seat as possible. If you are singled out, you can only try to keep calm, and pray. But whether you meet your maker with resignation, or whether you decide to try and take one of them with you is something no one can possibly advise on, particularly if the gun or knife is pointing at you, and your would-be murderer appears to be seconds from carrying out his threat.

Most incidents end after a gruelling ordeal of waiting by the terrorists realising there's nothing further to be gained, and capitulating. Occasionally, hi-jacks end in a shoot-out, with authorities storming the aircraft. Although it might be difficult if you're cramped into an economy class seat, try and get on to the floor if possible, as innocent passengers have been killed or injured either by not taking cover, or by trying to 'lend a hand'.

HITCH-HIKING by *Andrew Denton*

Of all the forms of travel available to explore a new country, none brings you into closer contact with the people and way of life than hitch-hiking. It's one of the oldest and simplest ways of moving about, and used by people from all walks of life the world over. Although hitch-hiking can be a fast method of travelling from A to B if done well, it's always a gamble, but that's part of the appeal. You stand by the road at the beginning of the day, and you can never be sure where you'll be at the end!

I was thumbing out of Jackson-Hole, Wyoming, once, heading for California. A truck pulled up, and an English voice yelled out, so I hopped up on the back. As we drove out of town, a story evolved. The owner of the voice, a lady, had to travel 180 miles south to Rock Springs, to catch a bus in order to get a plane home — and she had to be there in three and a half hours! The truck dropped us at the edge of town, and in my new role as bodyguard, I joined the lady heading south for Rock Springs. We made it by the skin of our teeth. She waved goodbye from the bus, leaving me in one of the most God-forsaken bus stations I've stood in, the rain pouring down, and night closing in, and two hundred miles off course! But it's the stuff travel is made of, and if you wanted things easy, you'd take the train — right?

I've hitched thousands of miles in many countries, and have never had any real problems, but that doesn't stop it being potentially dangerous. It's a sad sign of the times, but single ladies should think hard about hitching alone. Ken Welsh's 'Hitch Hikers Guide to Europe' is the bible for hitchers, and makes good background reading for a trip.

HYPOTHERMIA

These are the 'rules of thumb' for hitchers. Always try and look professional. Have a sign, your luggage (not too much), look neat, and as though you're really trying to get somewhere. No one wants to pick up a half asleep beatnik from the 60's! Always stand where you can be safely seen. Leave your pack, and walk down the road to look at it. If you were a driver, could you see it – and just as important, could you stop in time to pick up someone?

Check your lifts before you get in. If you can smell alcohol, or grass (marijuana), think carefully about what you're going to do. Whilst you and your pack are outside the car, you still have a choice. It all comes down to experience. Hitching is a sport, and although there is an element of luck, like any sport, you get better with practice. And remember, in those really desperate waits, something **always** turns up. It may be a long time coming, but no one ever stayed put for ever!

HYPOTHERMIA

The temperature of the human body is 36.9 degrees C. Unclothed, it would exist comfortably in still air at the same temperature. In cooler climates, we wear clothes to compensate for the heat loss which would otherwise take place. When the 'heat debt' gets too much, and the body starts losing heat more rapidly than it can be replaced, it starts to shut down the circulation to the less important parts of the body.

Hands and feet usually feel cold, and if the heat loss continues, the body shuts down more and more blood vessels beneath the skin, keeping all the warm blood pooled around the vital organs. The situation gets critical when the affected person starts to behave unreasonably. His speech becomes slurred, and his movements may become erratic. He could either complain of being cold and tired, or be filled with sudden violent outbursts of energy. He may also have difficulty focusing his eyes. If left untreated, the victim's temperature will fall lower, shivering will stop, and shortly afterwards, he'll drift into a coma and then die.

A good mountain leader can recognise the early symptoms of hypothermia, and should take immediate action. The most important thing is to get the patient into some form of shelter, whether tent, bivvy bag, survival bag, or just some natural feature like a rock outcrop. If possible, the patient should get into dry clothing and a sleeping bag, and then be given hot drinks (**NO** alcohol!)

If changing clothes is impractical, and in bad weather, it usually is, since the patient can lose even more body heat, he should be put into the sleeping bag as he is. If the bag is a down one, it should be lined with a plastic survival bag to prevent the wet clothes from impairing its insulation capability. Synthetic filled and fibre pile bags are much better in this respect, as they will still perform when wet. Ensure there's plenty of insulation between the patient and the ground (a Karrimat is best). If there's room in the sleeping bag, put another person in with the patient, to help keep him warm.

Provided you take adequate care, and don't let yourself get into a position where exhaustion can combine with cold and wet, you should never encounter a situation which might lead to hypothermia. I've had the misfortune to suffer it under relatively controlled circumstances, and I have to say that even mild hypothermia isn't pleasant. Prevention is by far the best course of action.

Critical body core temperatures:
37 degrees C – normal body core temperature
35 degrees C – first symptoms of hypothermia
33 degrees C – normal skin temperature
31 degrees C – unconscious, still responding to
                 stimulation
30 degrees C – coma
28 degrees C – death

INFORMATION

INFORMATION

When it comes to finding out information, whether it's about travelling times, or the location of the nearest hotel, shop, or chippie, you are to an extent in the hands of strangers. Somehow you need to be certain that whatever you find out is correct. Details about a country, where to find tourist attractions, and so on, are all things you can glean from tourist literature or books before you go.

If you have to ask someone a question, phrase it in such a way that he has to give you a proper answer, not just 'yes' or 'no'. In other words, ask 'which is the way to the railway station?' and not 'is that the way to the railway station?' I've discovered in many places that people don't like to appear unknowledgeable, so they tend to tell you anything rather than admit they don't know. It's a quaint custom, and illustrates well the need to double check any locally gleaned information several times.

Perhaps a little more amusing was the time in New Zealand when the road I was driving along petered out into one massive road works, and the single lane of dirt track was blocked for half an hour by a tanker re-fuelling various digging machines and a bulldozer. When I called the foreman over to establish exactly where I was, he kindly informed me in the very best ear-bending Strine that I was 'in a bloody great hole, mate!'

INSECT REPELLENT

The best active ingredient in insect repellents is Diethyl Toluamide — Deet, for short. Many brands of repellent actually have very little of the stuff in them, and are consequently not brilliantly effective. The best ones have concentrations between 80% and 95%. Repel 100 is about the most effective.

In the event of an emergency, I've been told that a 50/50 mix of Dettol and baby oil is very effective. No doubt it isn't just the insects that keep away! The other makeshift method of keeping the little blighters at bay is to use a cigarette. You'll gather elsewhere in this book that I'm an ardent anti-smokist, but there are times when a packet of fags can be useful. Offering them to those that want 'em can make friends, and get things done when you appear to be beset by an insurmountable problem. And even if you don't turn yourself blue puffing on them, I've found that holding a lighted cigarette can make quite a difference when you're being buzzed by clouds of insects.

You can get those fragile coils which smoulder gently, giving off insecticidal smoke to keep the little beggars away, and more recently, Spira have introduced a range of gadgets which plug into every known power socket, and gently cook tablets which produce fragrant bug-killing fumes. They also do a version for camping, using a tiny catalytic heater burning meths (note however that meths is not allowed in your luggage when travelling by air, and is not always readily available).

Every now and then, someone revives those little electronic devices which were supposed to repel mosquitoes by emitting a high-pitched whistle. The theory is that you're only bitten by female mosquitoes after they have mated, as they need blood to nourish the eggs. And once they have mated, they don't want males anywhere near them.

These penlight battery driven electronic wotsits are supposed to mimic the sound of male mosquitoes, and whilst apparently having been tested by all sorts of worthy organisations, I tried two models, and found them to be totally useless. What's more, with the whistle in a confined space like a small tent, the noise was downright irritating! I wasn't the only one to find out they were a load of rubbish. Following a successful action under the Trades Descriptions Act, they were withdrawn from sale, but it still hasn't stopped the things from re-appearing. This example of high technology is a waste of money.

INSURANCE – *See also Medical Treatment, Baggage*

If you book a holiday through a travel agent, it's likely you'll be offered travel insurance. Whether you take theirs, or organise your own, it's most advisable to cover yourself. And even if you're travelling under your own steam, you need the peace of mind that travel insurance affords. It might not be a case of claiming for delays or lost baggage. If you fall ill, or have an accident, medical charges can be extremely high. And because the facilities abroad may be a lot less than perfect, you want a policy that will cover the cost of evacuation by air ambulance. For that reason, it's not uncommon to find travel policies with sums insured up to £1 million.

EEC countries have reciprocal arrangements with the UK, where some or all of your medical costs are covered. To qualify, you have to present form E111, available from your local DHSS office, at the time of treatment. But the fact is that an E111 doesn't guarantee you the best treatment, and in many ways, it ensures you receive second class service. Good insurance offers peace of mind.

The reputable companies have an emergency 24

INSURANCE

hour telephone service. Make sure yours does, and use it if necessary. I met a chap who broke his legs whilst climbing in the Andes. How he made it back at all is another story, but when he eventually arrived in Lima, the hospital wouldn't operate on him until the insurance question was sorted out. It took two days!

Check that what you're doing is covered. Travel insurance has a standard winter sports exclusion, which can be brought under the umbrella of cover by paying an additional premium. But if you engage in anything dangerous, like technical climbing, hang-gliding or whatever, you will have to arrange special cover — if you can get it!

Travel insurance also covers baggage against loss or damage, along with money and other possessions like cameras. Check that the sums insured are sufficient. If you have a lot of expensive photographic equipment, you should have it insured anyway, and the cheapest way of doing it normally is by covering it under the all risks section of a house contents policy, and then paying a nominal extra premium to give world-wide cover for the duration of your trip (applies to non-professional photographers only). If you lose any belongings, or something is stolen, you should report the loss to the local police immediately, and retain a copy of your statement — the insurance company will need to see it as evidence of a valid claim.

JET-LAG – *See appendix for Time Differences*

Long haul flights crossing several time zones can be awfully confusing for your poor old body. You end up feeling ready for lunch when it's pitch dark, and tired when everyone else is bright and sparkling. The reason is that your circadian rhythms, the body's built-in clock which tells you when to wake up, when to be hungry, and when to go to sleep, is thrown out of joint. Add to that the tiring effect of air travel anyway, the dry cabin air, and lack of decent exercise, and you see why long distance air travel is so exhausting.

Some cope with it better than others, and it doesn't necessarily follow that the younger you are, the more able you are to handle this bombardment to your biological timekeeper. On shorter flights, the best way is probably to set your watch to the local time of your destination the moment you take off. It depends on how the airline serves the meals in-flight, though. At the least, be prepared for dinner at breakfast time, and various other permutations. If you eat just a little when each meal is served, you'll gradually disengage your body clock from its set rhythm, ready to impose another when you recover in your new time zone. Once you arrive in your new time zone, you should expect to take up to four or five days before you get completely used to new sleeping and eating times.

It's a good idea to give yourself a little exercise on a long flight. Stand up and walk around every now and then – it helps reduce swelling in the feet caused by blood pooling to the lower part of the body. And if the aircraft makes refuelling stops, take advantage of them to do a little more brisk walking. Even if it's only a dozen times around the transit lounge, it's a whole lot better than sitting down there too! Transit lounge trampers seem to number around 30% of a total flight (my estimate anyway), and you tend to find that those weed smokers just sit around in unfit heaps, polluting the air.

LANGUAGE

The fact that you're reading this book means that as a traveller, you have an unfair advantage wherever you go. You speak English. It's the most common international language, and the official tongue of airline pilots and air traffic controllers. It's a very unfortunate traveller that can't get by without sticking to English. All of which makes us an extremely lazy lot. Elsewhere in the world, it isn't uncommon for people to leave school speaking two or three languages fluently.

But once you get off the beaten track, it's very easy to come unstuck. Phrase books can be useful, provided they show you the correct pronunciations of whatever you're trying to blurt out. With a little extra time, you could try learning a few useful phrases from a tape. The Linguaphone courses are very good (they're also very expensive), but there are several others around which are more realistically priced, notably the ones by Berlitz. If you can spare the time, you can usually get a pretty good variety of courses at your local adult education centre.

In fact, these days, it doesn't even pay to advertise your nationality too openly. Britain's image abroad has suffered greatly in recent years at the hands of the moronic few whose collective intelligence can be summarised on a postage stamp. But whatever, you will find that your crude attempts at communicating with the locals in their mother tongue will endear you to them far more quickly than any contrived act of kindness.

LIGHTER

A small disposable butane gas lighter is a very useful thing to have with you, even if you don't smoke. It makes lighting camping stoves easy compared with the hassle of matches, which tend to blow out, get wet, or just break in two as you strike them. It also makes a useful provider of emergency light, and with ecology in mind, I always use mine to burn toilet paper when out in the wilds.

If you're travelling by air, you should carry the lighter on your person. It's regarded as dangerous if packed in your luggage, as there's the possibility that gas could leak out and consequently ignite.

LIGHTWEIGHT TRAVELLING

Of course, this whole book is devoted to the concept, but think for a moment just what you can do to lessen the load you take with you when travelling.

LIGHTWEIGHT TRAVELLING

Some of it comes down to attitude, and I suspect that vanity has a strong hand in things when people travel with several suitcases loaded down with several wardrobes of clothing — most of which probably won't be worn!

Start out with a sensible approach, and then adopt a ruthless one. Do you **really** need all those things you've packed. One well-known travel writer once advised people to take 'half the clothes, and twice the money' when they travelled. It's not a bad rule of thumb. Most people take more clothes than they need. If you've got a couple of changes, that's enough. Easy care clothing like Rohan's can be washed without any bother, so why take more than you need?

Look at the section on wash-bags, and you'll find some tips on how to cut down on weight in your toiletries. But the same principles can be applied in other areas. Mind you, you can get quite fanatical about it. Reinhold Messner, one of the mountaineers to first climb Everest without oxygen, is reputed to go as far as removing the labels from his underwear!

Further on in this A to Z, you'll find the section on lists. Listing the things you take with you on a trip unclutters the mind. It's easy to check you've got everything you need, and it eases the problems with possible insurance claims in the event of loss. But it also helps for a spot of post-trip analysis. Cross off the items you didn't use at all, or hardly used. You'll know not to take them next time.

If you're travelling entirely self-propelled, and carrying camping equipment, weight becomes an even more critical factor. Apart from the toiletries, covered under wash-bags, there are still a few other consumables where you can knock off some weight. The cardboard covers on Ordnance Survey maps each weigh just under an ounce. Not a lot perhaps, but what if you're carrying six maps? They're a lot easier to use without the covers, as well.

Similarly, any packaging which can be removed from food items should be disposed of. The cardboard wrap on something like a dehydrated meal might weigh what seems a paltry half an ounce, but on the basis of a two-man breakfast, main meal and individual desserts for a four-day supply, you can multiply that by sixteen — that's half a pound of cardboard! Do make sure you know what you've got, and how to prepare it, though. Write the details straight onto the plastic bags with a spirit-based fibre-tip pen, or use small sticky labels.

Things like coffee, dried milk and sugar can also be estimated fairly accurately for a lightweight camping trip, so no need to take whole jars if you don't need to. Use either poly-bottles, or even plastic bags, and measure out the number of spoonfuls you're likely to need. If you allowed for two or three brews a day, with one or two extra spoonfuls added for luck, you might still come out with less than a whole jar.

One of my few luxuries in terms of weight is my Thermarest sleeping mat, worth the extra weight for a comfortable night. If you use a full-length Karrimat, or similar closed-cell foam mat, you can save about five ounces by shortening it to three-quarter length. It's good enough for summer backpacking, and you can stop your feet getting cold by putting rucksack, pannier bags or spare clothes under them.

Rucksacks, with all their straps, are marvellous things for drying clothes — you should also bear this in mind if you have to pack up a tent soggy with condensation, rain, or both. A soaked flysheet, even a nylon one, could have **increased** its weight by a pound or more, so don't carry that extra weight to your next camp site. Strap the fly to your rucksack, and turn another part of it to the air every time you stop for a rest. Make sure that no guylines or parts of the fly are dangling, though. You don't want to trip over, or damage the tent by snagging it on something.

Finding ways of saving on luggage weight is an absorbing exercise. You can save a considerable amount by making pieces of kit double up on some functions — a waterproof jacket could be used as a general windproof, although you might find it a little uncomfortable in some conditions. If you can get by without a knife and fork, and use your spoon for eating and stirring tea, you can save another couple of ounces. Solo campers can dispense with a bowl, just eat straight out of the cooking pot! Of course, it's down to you as to where you want to draw the line, but it's fun once you start thinking about what you carry, and comparing it with what you actually need to carry.

LISTS

Unless you happen to have a computer for a brain, it pays to keep everything well-ordered with the help of a few lists. It starts before you set off, with a note of things you need to do or buy. A list of what items you pack in your luggage doesn't just help you sort out what you really need, and what you don't, it can also make any possible lost luggage claim a little easier to process. As I write, the point is all the more pertinent after having had a narrow escape with a wallet full of credit cards. It 'flew' out of my pocket in a busy shopping street in Auckland, in New Zealand, and I had to provide an accurate description of the contents when I reported the loss to the police. (I was very lucky. I got it back!)

List also the documents you need with you —

passport, tickets, visa, driving licence, travel insurance certificate. But unless you want to map out your travels in fine detail, I'd keep lists purely for practical items. It's much more fun to take the rest as it comes!

'That's a hell of a list you've got there, friend.'

MALARIA

MALARIA

Spread by the anopheline family of mosquitoes, malaria occurs in many tropical and sub-tropical areas of the world. There are different strains of the parasite, but generally, the symptoms in humans are high fever with alternate shivering and sweating, accompanied by intense headaches and nausea. It can be fatal, and at the least can cause long-term ill-health, as the illness will continue to recur.

People living in malarial areas tend to build up immunity if they survive childhood attacks of the disease. But westerners entering such areas have no immunity, and without any precautions, can easily fall prey to it. In 1985, over 2,000 British travellers returning home developed malaria, and five of the cases were fatal. There is no vaccination available, only prophylactic pills, taken daily and/or weekly. The course of tablets should allow you to start about a week before you set off, and should continue to be taken for four to six weeks after you return home.

There are further complications in that some strains of malaria in certain areas have built up resistance to anti-malaria drugs. It's important that you establish where you are going, and receive the correct tablets. If in doubt, contact the Malaria Reference Laboratory at the London School of Hygiene and Tropical Medicine. (See Appendix).

MAPS — See also Compass, Navigation

Poring over a map can be as absorbing as reading a good book, and it provides a lot of insight into the area you're visiting — providing you can read maps properly, of course. For general touring, a small scale map like 1:1,000,000 will probably show you major routes, towns and cities. If you need to navigate, either for walking or cycling, then large scale maps are advisable — the larger the better. Spend some time looking at maps, and get a feel for what they represent. Contour lines help you gauge more accurately what the terrain is like, how steep the hills are.

Stanfords in London is the best place to buy maps, particularly if you're after something a little more obscure. The Royal Geographical Society in Kensington Gore has an unrivalled map library, which is open to members of the society. One important point — if you're journeying to the more remote areas of the world, you must accept that mapping isn't up to Ordnance Survey standards. Either the surveys themselves will be very outdated, or they will merely be inaccurate through poor mapping. Either way, it should add a little spice to life, and keep you on your toes!

MEDICAL KIT — *See also First Aid*

Pain can be a very difficult concept to get across to someone who doesn't speak your language. I remember vividly going out for the day in Norway, leaving my first aid kit back at camp. As rotten luck would have it, I rekindled an old back injury, and there I was hobbling into the general store in the picturesque fjord-side village of Flåm, bent almost double with excruciating pain. Now if you've bruised or cut yourself, you can usually point to the injury, and they'll come up with something that stands a fair chance of working. I pointed to my back, and they kept producing jars of different ointments, when what I needed desperately was a powerful painkiller!

A general medical kit for travelling makes good sense, although if your need is dire, most ships, airliners, buses, and hotels may be able to come up with a plaster or an aspirin. Motion sickness on airliners is comparatively rare these days, as weather radar and higher cruising altitudes means that aircraft can avoid most of the turbulence which causes it. If conditions onboard ship are so severe that you need motion sickness tablets, there's a good chance fifty others will as well, and the queue for pills could be a long one! Rohan's Travelaid is a compact kit weighing just 250 grams, containing all the essential items you need, and which covers most travelling emergencies. The contents are as follows:

Analgesics   10

Treats headaches, rheumatic pains, toothache, and period pains. Also relieves the discomfort of colds and flu, chest and throat infections, and helps to lower temperature.

Diarrhoea treatment   9

Salt and Dextrose tablets. Stop food intake, and rehydrate with an electrolyte solution made from one tablet dissolved in a pint of water. If possible, let nature take its course, and keep up the fluid intake. On longer trips, this method of treatment will help your body build up a natural defence against the tummy bugs. If you run out, one teaspoon full of salt, and one of sugar mixed in a pint of water will do the same thing.

Anti-diarrhoea treatment   20

An added medication to actually glue up the works when things get desperate. If you're sitting on a bus for hours on end, you haven't much choice. The pills do only relieve the symptoms, however. As diarrhoea could itself be the symptom of something

more serious, you should take medical advice if it
persists for more than three days, or if it's accompanied
by severe stomach pains or fever.

Laxatives 10

Changes in routine and diet often give rise to
constipation, very common at the beginning of a
holiday.

Motion sickness tablets 10

Cyclizine, suitable for motion sickness during
road, rail, sea and air travel.

Anti-histamine tablets 10

Provide relief from the symptoms of rashes,
bites, stings and oedema. Also useful for treating
allergic reactions. Anti-histamine tablets can cause
drowsiness, so shouldn't be used if driving, and the
effect of the tablet is increased by alcohol.

Indigestion tablets 12

Gives quick relief from indigestion, heartburn
and nervous indigestion.

Throat lozenges 15

Relieves sore throats, gumboils and mouth
infections such as ulcers. Can be used as a mouth
antiseptic after tooth extractions.

Savlon antiseptic cream 1 tube

For cuts and grazes. Prevents infection.

Insect repellent 1 stick

Use on arms, legs and face to prevent insect
bites.

Sterile swabs 2

Used to clean cuts and grazes before dressing.

Non-adherent dressing 1
Plasters 6
Bandage 1
Garment repair 1 kit
Instruction booklet
Scissors

You may need to supplement the basic kit with
anything else for your particular needs – anti-malarial
tablets, vitamin pills, or whatever. If you're taking
treatment for a medical condition, make absolutely
certain that you have enough supplies with you to last
the duration of your trip.

MEDICAL TREATMENT – See also Insurance

It's all very well being insured, but what do you
actually do if you fall ill, or suffer the misfortune of an
accident? Whatever the problem, get the medical
treatment first. In the normal run of things, you would
be expected to pay for your treatment, and then
submit a claim on the medical expenses section of your
travel insurance.

But obviously, if you have a major problem, and

there's no way you could settle the bill yourself, you should make sure that the medical people you consult see your insurance certificate. Someone should then contact your insurers on the emergency telephone number as soon as possible. Similarly, if you are somewhere where medical facilities are inadequate, and your condition is serious, arrangements should be made without delay to evacuate you by the fastest means possible, either by repatriating you, or getting you to the nearest decent hospital.

MONEY – *See also Credit Cards, Travellers Cheques*

Needs taking care of in large amounts, but in most places, still the most acceptable form of payment. In fact if you tender a strong currency such as Sterling or US dollars, you may find it more desirable than the local lolly. It's useful to keep a certain amount of currency with you to pay for expenses like taxis, bus fares and food. Make sure you keep the receipts when you exchange your sterling into local currency, as invariably you'll be required to produce them in order to reconvert any remaining currency back to sterling.

Countries with weak currencies, such as those in the Eastern bloc, and third world countries, often have thriving currency black markets, where you could be offered anything up to four times the official rate for your Sterling or Dollars. Very advantageous to the traveller, but ever so slightly illegal, of course. You also need to weigh it against how much currency you're really likely to spend. Many countries with strict controls require foreigners to pay such things as hotel bills in foreign currency.

MONEY BELT

Useful piece of kit for the security conscious, used not just for money, but passports and other important documents as well. Make sure you get one with a soft cotton backing. Nylon is extremely uncomfortable in hot weather. It's also advisable to keep a small float of money for everyday use in a purse or wallet in another secure pocket. It can be quite alarming for a shopkeeper to see his customer apparently on the verge of stripping off when purchasing goods!

MOTION SICKNESS – *See also Medical Kit*

A disturbance of the inner ear which can occur in all forms of transport. Even England's greatest sailor, Nelson, suffered from it! You can avoid it, or at least

MOTION SICKNESS

lessen the effects, by choosing your position carefully. On board ship, the movement is more accentuated at the bow and stern (sharp and blunt ends for the non-nautical), and on the higher decks. Get yourself somewhere amidships. On a bus or coach, anywhere beyond the line of the rear wheels is likely to give trouble if you're susceptible. Sit as near to the front as you can. On an airliner, the tail end of the plane is most likely to give rise to any motion sickness. It's also true to say that a lot of motion sickness is self-induced, either by the excitement of going away on holiday, or from anxiety.

If you are likely to suffer from motion sickness, you should avoid taking alcohol, and lay off the fatty foods. Take a motion sickness tablet a minimum of 20 to 30 minutes before your departure. Leave it until you're actually being sick, and the tablet won't be absorbed.

NAVIGATION – *See also Maps, Compass*

Using a map and compass is definitely the easiest way of navigating, but there could be times when you might be caught out. So it pays to have a trick or two up your sleeve. The following are a few methods of establishing a north/south line:

1. During the day, you can use your watch, provided it's set to the correct local time. Point the hour hand towards the sun. Halfway between the hour hand and 12 o'clock is a line pointing south, if you're in the northern hemisphere. If you're in the southern hemisphere, the line will be pointing to the north. Got a digital watch? Well, don't despair. Just draw a clock with the correct time, and carry on as before. Not brilliantly accurate, but a good rough guide.

2. Again, if you have the correct local time, the shadow of an upright stick planted in the ground at 12 noon will give you a north/south line. Once again, remember the line will point south in the northern hemisphere, and north in the southern hemisphere.

3. If you don't have a watch, or it has somehow been put out of action, the only other way involves spending a bit of time in one place. Plant a pole upright in the ground, and, starting off in the morning, mark the top of the pole's shadow on the ground at intervals throughout the day. At the end of the day, draw a line connecting the points to give you an east/west line. The shortest distance from the base of the pole to the line (which will be the position at noon) will give you the north/south line. Same directions as before regarding hemispheres.

4. At night, you can do as the early navigators did, and use the stars. In the northern hemisphere, the Pole Star indicates true north. First of all, find the constellation of the Plough, or Great Bear, as it's more correctly known. It looks vaguely like a saucepan, and the key stars are the two furthest from the handle. An imaginary line drawn upwards roughly five times the distance between those two stars will take you to the Pole Star.

In the southern hemisphere, you look for another constellation, the Southern Cross. It's a group of four stars in a diamond pattern, and a line drawn through the top and bottom stars points approximately south. To the left of the constellation are two bright stars, and a line drawn at right angles between the two points directly south.

PACKING

PACKING

Why have a section on packing? It's self explanatory, isn't it? Well, it does help to point out that when you pack your luggage, you should bear two things in mind — weight distribution, and the positioning of fragile/sharp objects. Anyone used to a rucksack will know that it feels far more comfortable and stable with all the high density (heavy) objects packed towards the back of the sack, so the main body of weight is as close to the wearer's centre of gravity as possible.

You can't do quite the same with a suitcase, but you can make sure it balances naturally from the handle, which in turn will save straining your arm unduly. Suitcases on wheels trundle more easily with the heavier objects arranged so they're at the bottom when the suitcase is standing on its wheels. Soft luggage users should pack so that sharp or fragile objects are well protected in the main bulk of clothing. About the only airline I've used which provides a sturdy plastic crate for individual items of soft luggage is British Airways. (If there are more, let us know).

You can help to minimise the chances of a rucksack or other soft luggage coming unstuck with a little thought beforehand. Pack it so that there are no awkward lumps near the outside. Items of clothing will also help protect anything more fragile which can be packed in the middle. You should also try to make sure you don't have any loose straps. If you can remove the hip-belt, pack it inside the sack. Failing that, you should wrap it backwards around the pack, do up the buckle, tighten the strap, and tuck in the end. Shoulder straps should be adjusted tight, with the trailing straps tucked in or wound around themselves. Similarly, the loose ends of profile straps should be tucked away, and any removable accessory fastenings such as crampon straps taken off. I very nearly lost the top of a rucksack once when the check-in clerk lifted it onto the conveyor belt by the nearest thing to hand — one crampon strap!

Airlines provide lists of articles which may not be taken as luggage on board an aircraft, and they include any pressurised containers such as aerosols or gas containers, corrosive chemicals, flammable and explosive substances. But even the more innocuous things need a little care. Make sure that the caps on your various toiletries are screwed on tight, and play safe by putting them in a separate plastic bag, just in case of spills. I have to confess to opening my travel bag on one occasion to a shampoo sodden collection of clothing!

Plastic bags don't just protect your luggage from the seeping horrors inside your luggage. In fact, it's best to pack everything inside plastic bags. Experienced backpackers always use a large heavy duty bag as a liner for their rucksacks, and the same is true with cycle panniers. Prolonged heavy rain seeps through the stitching of such luggage, so an extra line of defence is a good precaution. The same goes if your bag or case is likely to be tied to a vehicle roof rack, where rain is even more likely to penetrate an unprotected bag or case.

PASSPORT

The quickest form of documentation for a trip abroad is the 1 year Visitor's passport, which is valid for most European countries. It is a temporary thing, though, and you'll find that it won't be acceptable for any visits to countries where you need a visa.

Like Visitor's Passports, application forms for five or ten year passports can be picked up from Post Offices, but the completed form, with references, inside leg measurements and all the rest, has to be sent off to your local passport office. You should allow at least four weeks for your application to be processed, and preferably more if you apply during the busy summer months. In cases of extreme urgency (and you would need to produce your travel documents to prove it really was urgent), you can apply in person either at your local passport office, or the main one in London. A joint passport can be issued to cover husband and wife, although only the husband (if he happens to be the first named on the passport) can use it to travel alone.

1987 saw the introduction of the standardised EEC format of passport to Britain, with the name 'European Community' taking precedence over that of the issuing country. And in line with the increasing use of computers at immigration points, it features a machine readable magnetic strip. The plum coloured passport will still bear the traditional coat of arms, however.

Your passport is a valuable document, and could be misused if it fell into unscrupulous hands. It goes without saying that you should keep it with you at all times when you travel abroad, and to simplify things in the event of losing it, you should always keep a separate note of the passport number, and the date and place of issue.

Officials on immigration desks traditionally have this rather dour image, but I've cracked it. As a typical example of the eccentric travelling Englishman, I go everywhere with my four inch tall travelling teddy, Bill. As one would reasonably expect, Bill has his own passport (obtained from the International Teddy Bear

Club), and which I present for stamping everywhere we go. It's fun collecting the stamps, and momentarily driving a wedge through the seemingly impenetrable shell of bureaucracy.

In fact, there have been moments of unashamed favouritism, like in New Zealand, where Bill received work and permanent residence permits, which was more than I got! There have been the occasional problems, of course. The East Germans wouldn't stamp it (visa problems, I think), and the Finns made him go through the X-Ray machine on his own — a traumatic experience for any bear!

PHOTOGRAPHY — See also Camera, Film

Without doubt the one thing which most travellers have in common is photography, whether it's to capture the atmosphere of a place with a carefully conceived study of people or places, or just holiday snaps. The choice of cameras, lenses and films is dealt with elsewhere. By applying a little thought every time you reach for your camera, even beginners can take photographs they'll be proud of.

In normal lighting situations, a camera's metering system will provide a perfectly exposed photograph, and whether your camera has auto-focusing, or whether you focus the lens yourself, it's reasonable to assume that you should be able to get sharp pictures. The thing that needs working on is the way you compose your masterpieces.

First of all, don't get carried away when you see a view. Think about it. It's all too easy to snap away at what you see as an awe-inspiring vista, only to be disappointed when it appears lost in the photograph. Cultivate a bit of selectivity, and instead of trying to capture an expansive sweep of landscape, go for an aspect of detail. You could try positioning yourself so that you get something interesting in the foreground — a commonly used technique to add depth to the picture.

Although the metering systems of modern cameras are pretty foolproof, they do still need a bit of brainwork behind them to ensure correctly exposed photographs. For example, in snow, or on a sunny beach, where there's a great deal of reflected light, the meter will deliver a photograph which is under-exposed. The reason for that is that it sees all that reflected glare, and compensates for it. The answer is to fool the meter, either by using the exposure compensation facility which many cameras have these days, or by changing the film speed setting on your camera. If you want to set the camera to over expose a picture, you select a lower speed than the actual film speed. If you want to under expose a picture, then set a higher film speed. It's proportional, so every time you double the film speed, you under expose a stop — every time you halve the film speed, you over expose a stop.

For instance, if you were shooting ISO 100 film, and you wanted to over expose a scene by two stops, you would set it to ISO 25. These techniques are used on automatic cameras — if you have a manual camera, or an automatic with manual override, you would simply set a wider aperture or slower shutter speed than the one indicated by your meter. The other method with a manual camera is to meter off something with average reflectance when the overall scene is either very light or very dark. When shooting in bright snow scenes, I find the easiest method is to meter off the back of my hand, and take whatever is indicated as the exposure for the scene.

Despite whatever personal views you may hold about British weather, it is on the whole very good for nice even lighting in photographs. The clouds diffuse the light, and allow a much subtler range of colours to show. In hot, sunny places, the problem tends to be the extreme contrast between parts of a scene lit by sunshine, and the parts in shadow. Unless you're doing a close-up portrait where you can bring a bit of light into the shadow by using flash or a reflector, you have to accept that you can either expose one part of the scene correctly, with the other part either over or under exposed, depending on whether you went for the light or shade, or trying to draw a compromise. The fail-safe method is to 'bracket' exposure, shooting one frame at the exposure indicated by the meter, and then opening up one or two stops.

POCKET KNIFE

Most travellers like to capture their favourite moments and places on film. Problems can arise in certain parts of the world when you point your lens at military bases. It can even be quite amusing, when a 'sensitive' airfield is the base for just three or four ageing jets. Whatever you might think, you can still find yourself attracting the unwelcome attentions of the local constabulary — civilian, military, secret or whatever.

But it doesn't stop there. In some countries, it's forbidden to photograph public buildings, and in Northern India, where the border region with Tibet is particularly sensitive, I discovered you aren't allowed to take pictures of bridges, obviously of strategic importance. But where there's no apparent reason for prohibiting it, I have found attitudes are changing. In East Berlin, all I attracted were one or two rather strange looks when I climbed a building site fence to photograph a magnificent church in process of restoration.

POCKET KNIFE

A pocket knife can be a very handy thing to have with you. The best is without doubt the distinctive red-handled Swiss Army knife, although there are so many cheap and nasty copies around these days, you have to check closely. The foolproof way of finding out is to look at the base of the main blade on the knife. A genuine Swiss Army knife bears the name 'Victorinox', and the Swiss symbol of excellence, the crossbow.

There are lots of different models available, from basic ones with just a couple of blades, to the Champion, which has 53 different blades and tools, and includes a small pen, tweezers, corkscrew, screwdriver, files, blades for cutting and sawing, and plenty more besides.

Victorinox's proud boast is that without a Swiss Army knife, the 1975 Everest Expedition might not have been the success it was. Dougal Haston's oxygen system iced up at a crucial point in the climb, and it was Doug Scott's Swiss Army knife which removed the obstruction, and allowed them to become the first Brits to reach the summit.

And for lesser mortals, a pocket knife is just as much appreciated when it's really needed. Knives, files, tin and bottle openers all seem to come in very handy. And whilst they're called pocket knives, the pocket isn't the best place for one when you're passing through airport security. I sometimes think that airport metal detectors are so sensitive that the fillings in your teeth would set the bells and bleepers off. They most certainly react to even the smallest pocket knife, and because such things, along with apparently harmless scissors, are these days regarded as dangerous weapons, you may not be allowed to carry it with you. Best bet is to keep it packed at the bottom of your bag till you arrive at your destination.

POTS 'N PANS

The simple answer for lightweight campers is to take the very least you can get away with. If you're only using one stove, it doesn't make sense to carry more than one pot. A good aluminium billy will serve as your kettle, saucepan and bowl for eating. The lid keeps the steam in when you're cooking, can be used as a frying pan when required, and serves as a side plate for cold food eaten with your meal. Don't buy pots with built-in folding handles. They're rarely efficient, and if you do use more than one pot, you're carrying unnecessary weight. Better to use a light alloy pot gripper which can be used on all. The best you can get is made by Trangia.

The billy should have a good rolled over lip around the top so your gripper can work safely, and a reasonably wide radiused curve from the side to the bottom of the pot. Tight corners make it more difficult to keep spotlessly clean. Trangia and Sigg both make extremely good billies. If you're camping two up, then you'll obviously have to use something else from which to eat your food. A plastic bowl is much easier to use in the confines of a tent than a plate.

Don't forget just how much space you have inside your pot when packing your rucksack or pannier. It's the ideal place to put anything that ought not to be squashed. Make sure that things can't move about inside, though. Rattling noises from within your luggage can be infuriating!

PREPARATION

Not just down to deciding what clothes and other odds and ends you take with you, or sorting out what visas and tickets you need. If you're taking camping equipment, make sure it's all in good order. Same thing if you're travelling with a bicycle or car. It also pays to have a dry run with any equipment like a stove, tent or camera which is either new, or with which you're unfamiliar.

Footwear needs to be comfortable, so take new, unworn shoes or boots at your peril! Try different ways of packing your luggage until you're happy with the way it feels when you carry it, and that you can get to the things which need to be accessible without pulling everything else out.

PRICKLY HEAT

It's not a bad idea to take the same attitude with yourself. If your travels are likely to involve exertion which you're not accustomed to, whether it's trekking, skiing or cycle touring, a bit of training will get you into shape, and thus enable you to enjoy your trip that much more.

PRICKLY HEAT

An irritating rash which can develop in hot climates. It occurs where profuse sweating doesn't evaporate quickly enough, and the pores get blocked, usually where clothing is rather tight. You can prevent it by wearing loose-fitting clothes in hot climates, and taking reasonable opportunities to cool off in a bath or shower. If you do get a bad case of prickly heat, try and stay in the cool if possible (and so avoid making your sweat glands work). Wash frequently in cold water, and without soap. Anti-histamine tablets will provide relief from bad irritation.

PUBLIC HOLIDAYS

Wherever you travel, it pays to check that there isn't a public holiday on what might be the one and only day you pass through civilisation, hoping to find a bank or shops. It can work in your favour though, because you might find yourself joining in the celebrations of some colourful festival.

RABIES

Fortunately, tight controls on the movement of animals into Britain has meant that this terrible disease has so far been kept at bay. But it is widespread in parts of Europe, and further afield, particularly India and parts of Africa. It can be spread by any animal, but chiefly by dogs. A human contracts the disease by being bitten, or even by a scratch or graze being licked by a rabid animal. Once the symptoms of rabies appear, the disease is always fatal.

If you happen to be bitten by an animal in a country where rabies is known to occur, you should seek medical attention immediately, even if the animal appears to be healthy.

The wounds should be washed thoroughly with soap and water, but not scrubbed, which could actually assist the infection to penetrate. If possible, the wound should be flushed with fast flowing water from a tap or stream — the idea being to remove any excess saliva from the wound before it has a chance to be absorbed.

The incubation period is a minimum of 30 days, so there's generally time to get to a hospital to start the course of anti-rabies injections. It is possible to have a rabies inoculation, which although it doesn't give 100% protection, does extend the safe period for getting to a place where rabies serum can be administered. At the moment, it's still quite expensive, around £50, so is really only worth having if you're in an affected area for an extended visit, or doing veterinary work with possible carriers.

RADIO — *See appendix for short wave frequencies*

Some of my travelling friends go the whole hog, and take Sony's super-duper ICF 7600D portable synthesised scanning receiver, which picks up virtually everything from the BBC World Service to exploding super-novae (all right, not quite!) But at around 1¼ lbs, even that's a little heavy for me. For travelling at home and in Europe, I take one of those dinky little credit card sized FM radios. They're dirt cheap, but if you feel like splashing out a little extra, you can get one which picks up AM as well. Useful for tuning in for weather forecasts if you're walking the wild lands, they do have their drawbacks in that they aren't powerful enough to pick up transmissions very well inside buses, trains or other moving metal containers.

REPAIRS

The hardened traveller knows a thing or two about running repairs, whether it's the simple stuff like

RUCKSACKS

---

bunging the odd button back onto clothing, or more ingenious bits of makeshift mending on ailing rucksacks, or broken bicycles. A small kit with needle and thread is essential, but consider also a small tube of contact adhesive, which can be used to dope leaky seams in waterproof clothing, tents, rucksacks and cycle panniers. Superglue can be bought in very tiny tubes and bottles, so could also make a handy addition to any repair kit. A small piece of PU coated nylon can be used as a patch on all sorts of things — although you can also use self adhesive tape. Gaffa tape is the best, a fabric tape with super-strong adhesive, used by electricians, and rock bands for sticking myriads of microphone and speaker wires to the floor. Very good stuff for all sorts of emergency repair.

RUCKSACKS

Damned good things, whether you're going backpacking, travelling or shopping. After all, why burden yourself with the misery of lugging a suitcase, or even the inconvenience of a shoulder bag, for that matter, when you can strap your luggage to your back, and take the weight off your arms.

Rucksacks have come light years from the old canvas Bergens with steel frames and leather straps. External frame rucksacks make good load carriers, particularly if you're carrying about three weeks' supplies into the wilderness. But they don't travel very well. The frame can get caught up with other luggage, and I have to say I've seen some pretty mangled examples at the end of flights. They tend to be a bit cumbersome on other forms of public transport too.

In fact, you'd have to look hard to find a decent external frame rucksack these days. Firms like Karrimor and Berghaus have turned rucksack design into a cross between art and science, and certainly the products obtainable now are a far cry from the rucksacks of even ten or fifteen years ago.

Those designed for backpacking have hip-belts as well as shoulder straps, probably the biggest contribution to comfort, efficiency and safety. The majority of the weight acts upon the pelvis rather than the spine, which means that the spinal column is able to retain the correct posture, and thus avoid the risk of injury. (Perhaps we should be calling ourselves hip-packers? Yeah, man!) Rigid external frame rucksacks were a step in the right direction, although the fact that they held the load away from the back meant that the centre of gravity wasn't at the ideal point for carrying, so the load lacked stability. Whilst they still have their limitations, modern internal frame rucksacks fulfil the major requirements for a load-carrying system which is safe, comfortable and stable.

To get a load as close as possible to the line of your own centre of gravity, you have to shape the internal frame of the rucksack to the natural curve of your spine. Very comfortable, but with one major drawback! This is where the frame sack scored, because there isn't enough room for air to circulate and evaporate the inevitable perspiration. At the very least, you end up with a wet back, and if you forget to cover up when you remove the pack, there's the possibility of getting a chill to your back muscles, which in turn can lead to strains. Whilst climbing sacks sacrifice all for the sake of stability, backpacking sacks tend to be more of a compromise. Each manufacturer has his own method of allowing air to circulate behind the back, whilst still trying to keep the lines as body-hugging as possible.

By far the most significant development in rucksack design in recent years has been the adjustable harness. Previous to this, you had to buy a rucksack to fit to get a comfortable carry. The heavier the load in this sort of sack, the more you found it didn't quite feel right in all situations. The adjustable harness allows you to alter the back length of the sack, the distance between the hip-belt and the shoulder straps. Karrimor Condor and Berghaus Laser rucksacks use a stepless form of adjustment using straps which are very good for 'fine tuning'. The Berghaus AB system uses a rack of notches which allows the shoulder harness to be anchored in one of several positions. It hasn't quite got the range of adjustments that the Condor has, but for all that, the AB system offers excellent stability — essential when traversing tricky ground or in high winds. The much copied Lowe Paralux shoulder harness adjusts by moving a buckle along an anchored strap, with a sort of lattice of stitched-in straps to provide the variation in back lengths.

Cotton duck has all but disappeared from the scene as a rucksack material. It can take a lot of battering, but it's very heavy, even more so when water-logged. Then of course it takes on the attributes of hardboard when the temperature drops. Nylon is durable, and very receptive to waterproof coatings, but does lack a certain visual appeal. Cordura is a 'texturised' nylon fabric which has all the pleasant characteristics of cotton, but much lighter, and with the hard-wearing performance of nylon. Most manufacturers offer sacks in this material.

The choice is vast, and the different types and their applications fall outside the scope of this book. But for general backpacking and travel, a two compartment sack with side pockets, capacity around 75 litres, would serve pretty well. Make sure you've got one with a padded hip-belt, unless your hips have good natural padding!

SAFETY DRILL

Most of the people I see on an aircraft take scant notice of the safety drill which the cabin crew are obliged to run through at the beginning of every flight. Maybe they know exactly what to do in the event of an emergency, but I suspect not. The only time any safety procedures are carried out on boats is on the first day of a long cruise. The short haul ferries have no such procedures, and in the light of the Zeebrugge ferry disaster, there may well be some changes, although the speed of that particular accident was such that there was no time to do anything.

If nothing else, you should know how to put a life jacket on, and you should find out where your nearest emergency exit is. That latter applies whether you happen to be in an aircraft, bus or hotel. Remember, there could just be a day when you have to use it for real, and the chances are it will be in the dark!

SANITATION

Where toilet facilities leave a lot to be desired, or where you haven't any at all, the most important thing is to make sure you wash your hands thoroughly before preparing or eating food. It's one of the commonest ways of getting a tummy upset. Typical French 'hole in the ground' loos aren't too bad once you've got used to them. One of the most distasteful toilet customs I've come across was in Greece, where their expertise in plumbing and sanitation is about as advanced as a council estate of mud huts. You aren't allowed to flush toilet paper down the loo, for fear of blocking the pipes, so you have to drop it into a waste paper basket placed next to the toilet. The bins were emptied regularly, every three days or so!

I remember stopping off at a small café in Tunisia, dying for a pee, and making a beeline (peeline?) for a door sporting a sign most obviously indicating that it was a toilet. Inside, to my horror, the porcelain bowl looked as though someone had tossed a hand grenade into it, and the floor surrounding the shattered bog was covered in great piles of what should have gone down the toilet. I went behind a wall outside. Gents have few problems when it comes to attending to such matters, particularly if it is just a case of nipping over to the nearest tree. Ladies have to work slightly harder to preserve their dignity, but when all else fails, a brolly can make an effective screen.

You need to cultivate a certain amount of thick skin when it comes to toilet matters off the beaten track. I was caught short at the top of the Kuari Pass in the Himalayas, with an attack of diarrhoea. It was a knife edge ridge of snow, with absolutely nowhere to perform my miserable deed out of sight of the eighteen other trekkers and forty porters. But as toilets go, it had one hell of a view!

SECURITY

Travellers tend to be rather vulnerable, even when travelling on their own, and seemingly in control of their own destinies. Unless you exist on hand baggage, there will come times when your luggage has to be entrusted to others. On board ships, and unless you have a cabin, if your luggage is big and heavy, you may have to lock it away for the duration of the voyage – not a bad thing, providing you keep a small bag with all your toiletries etc.

There was a time when you would have been straining your eyes to see an honest baggage handler at Heathrow, when organised baggage nobbling was in vogue. These days, things are much better, but it pays not to put temptation in front of anyone. Use padlocks and straps to make things difficult for would-be thieves.

As far as airport security is concerned, ours is as good as you'd expect to find anywhere. Some airlines such as Air India and El Al also institute extra checks, so that by the time you take your seat on the aircraft, you can be certain that every reasonable precaution has been taken to ensure the safety of the flight.

The only time when a hotel management will accept liability for your valuables is when they're deposited in the hotel safe. Very large hotels have been known to have resident burglars, and they know all the tricks when it comes to finding the things you thought you'd hidden away. There's a limit on how careful you can be, of course, but on no account should you ever leave money and passport in your hotel room. There are a number of locking boxes containing alarms available these days, and other alarms which can either be attached to your valuables, or even to the handle of your hotel room door at night. They all work on roughly the same principle, using a sensitive mercury activated switch to detect the slightest movement, thus setting off a piercing electronic squeal.

Many Asian hotels have a quaint way of locking guests' doors – you get a flimsy padlock, which nine times out of ten can be opened by every other key in the hotel – or failing that, can be sprung open by using a bit of judicious violence with a screwdriver. It's not such a daft idea to have your own sturdy padlock for times like these.

You're vulnerable to pickpockets and sneak

SECURITY

thieves when you're out and about, either sight-seeing, or at busy places like railway stations and airports, when your mind is concentrating on other things. They work on the basis of being able to distract you, so they can slip their hands into your pocket or shoulder bag when your attention is elsewhere. So pockets with zipped fastenings are the order of the day. Otherwise, you can use a money belt. Unfortunately, as a rather skinny person, I find a money belt containing passport and all those other essentials tends to be rather obtrusive worn under a shirt, and I don't find it particularly comfortable, especially when it's hot.

Of course, some criminals may be more brazen about it. Rome is famous for its motor scooter thieves, who have turned the removal of shoulder bags and other hand-carried items into an art-form. I remember the story about the lady whose rich husband had just bought her a very expensive fur coat in a large store. It was too hot to wear, and as she walked out into the street with the coat draped over her arm, the pillion passenger on a motor scooter whisked it away within minutes of the purchase. Serve her right for buying fur!

Shoulder bags make inviting targets, because thieves find them so easy to work on. What do you mean, it's always zipped up tight? A razor blade or sharp knife is the favoured tool here, and used either to slice the shoulder strap so the whole bag can be whipped away, or the cunning ones will actually slice into the bottom of your bag without your knowledge – they may even be chatting to you whilst they rob you blind! If you use a shoulder bag, make sure it isn't a cheap one made of thin nylon. A bag made of 12 ounce Cordura rucksack material is tougher to slice through, giving you the opportunity to discover what's going on. What you do after that depends on who's biggest!

The moral of the story is to keep your money and valuable documents about your person at all times, preferably in zipped pockets or a money belt. Putting all your eggs into one basket is potentially disastrous. The only items of value you should carry in your luggage are ones you wouldn't mind losing too much if the whole lot was pinched – in other words, stuff which can easily be replaced. The loss of money can be recovered through insurance, but it can be damned inconvenient in the meantime.

Keep your main supply of money in a money belt, and don't access it in anything other than total privacy. Your wallet containing one or two days' supply of cash should be in your front trouser pocket – never in your hip pocket, or in a jacket which you might take off – and preferably zipped. It's the most difficult place to pickpocket – try it! This way, if you happen to be mugged, you can send your attacker off with something without him causing you any injury because you resisted handing over your valuables.

If you are threatened by a mugger, don't argue, don't plead, and don't fight. Give him your wallet, and drop it on the floor — in fright, of course. When he bends down to pick it up — no, don't beat him round the head — RUN!

Danger to the person can stem from your nationality, so play safe, and don't advertise where you're from. More commonly, it comes from sexual motives or offence taken. Don't discuss religion, politics or football with anyone. If someone does try to draw you into a controversial conversation, claim ignorance. Nobody gets angry with numbskulls, but everybody hates a smartass! And chaps, don't pass remarks (good or bad) about any girl you clap eyes on. She's bound to be someone's sister!

Sexual dangers (see Women Travellers) don't automatically become the sole preserve of female travellers. Fellow publisher Paul Howcroft was given a really hard time by a 'gentleman' in a Venice cinema, once. 'Fortunately,' he says, 'I was bigger than he was and emerged with my honour intact.' But for travelling girls, sexual harassment in some form or other is a real possibility.

At the root of it all is the fact that, try as hard as you like, you can't appear inconspicuous. If you look like a traveller, the local felons will spot you a mile off. And on the basis of not being able to hide the fact, I don't even try. It's much better to dress for comfort, and take sensible precautions over security. Wander into the red light district, dubious clubs, or down some shady back alley on your own at night, and you're asking for trouble. Keep to places with plenty of people when you're out and about in towns and cities, and keep passport and money about your person at all times.

SHORTS

Damned useful things in warm weather, but if you're using them for extra ventilation rather than showing off your lovely legs (men or women), make sure they're not too tight fitting. Running shorts are cut ideally for this, but they don't have any pockets, and they don't really fall within the bounds of modesty. Purpose designed poly/cotton shorts are much better. It follows that if it's hot enough to wear shorts, you aren't likely to cocoon yourself in a jacket. If you're wearing just a T-shirt on top, the zipped pockets on Rohan shorts come in rather useful. And unlike most typical 'Doctor Livingstone, I presume' safari models, Rohan shorts pack ridiculously small.

Modesty is an important point, as I discovered

SHOULDER BAGS

when I turned up at a Jewish synagogue on the island of Djerba, in Tunisia. It was damned hot, and I was wearing shorts, T-shirt and trainers. The ladies with me were already covering their heads and arms with large Arab headscarves. The wizened old man at the door made it clear I wouldn't be allowed in dressed as I was, and reached for a large headscarf. I tied it around my waist in a skirt. What made this fetching little number so amusing was the fact that my head covering was a battered bush hat, and that I also had a number of camera pouches hanging from a prototype harness system. The effect? A very fetching sort of Eighth Army Desert Rat in drag!

SHOULDER BAGS

Used by many as cabin baggage, and as a weekend bag. Quite often they come as a free gift when you buy tickets. The main thing that seems to be wrong with shoulder bags, or at least the ones that I see, are that the shoulder straps are often very flimsy, and tend to part company with the bag at the least convenient moment.

SLEEPING BAGS – *See also Sleeping Mats*

No self-respecting traveller goes without a sleeping bag, at least not unless he plans on living in hotels or boarding houses. Quite obviously essential for camping, a sleeping bag can also come in very handy for making long waits in cold and draughty stations a bit more tolerable. Indeed, there are some so-called hotels I've stayed in where I've been glad to have a lightweight sleeping bag, where the bedding has looked distinctly dubious.

Never skimp when it comes to buying a sleeping bag. If you don't sleep comfortably, you certainly won't get any enjoyment out of your travelling. Insulation is the name of the game. The body is constantly producing and giving off heat, and the moment you start losing heat at a greater rate than it's produced, you feel cold. A good sleeping bag slows down this heat loss to a balance by providing a layer of insulation.

Just like double glazing, the best means of insulation is a layer of still air. The way a sleeping bag does this is with its filling, the fine filaments of down or synthetic fibres trapping pockets of air. Poor quality of filling, or just less filling, traps less still air, and consequently doesn't insulate so well. Broadly speaking, there are two main types of filling, natural and synthetic, and a range of qualities is available in each.

Down is the plumage with fluffy tendrils obtained from the breasts of water fowl. A certain number of feathers are always present as well, and the quality of the down depends on just what proportion of feathers have been removed. Down is allowed up to 15% feathers before it has to be called feather and down, rather than pure down. For efficiency, it beats all other forms of insulation hands down (get it?) — for any given weight of insulation, down provides more warmth than a synthetic filling. It's also more compressible, and has the ability to return its loft after a period of being packed much longer than any man-made material. A synthetic bag will last in average use three to five years, with its performance gradually deteriorating as the fibres lose the 'spring' which enable them to provide the insulating loft.

So a down bag can be made much lighter for any given value of insulation. It does have disadvantages as well, although sensible use can minimise them. Down loses its effectiveness when it becomes damp. The furry tendrils clump together, and no longer trap warm air, and once in this state, they take a long while to dry out. The answer here is not to let your sleeping bag get wet in the first place. The stuff sacks supplied with the majority of sleeping bags aren't waterproof, so bung the whole thing into a plastic bag as well. Use seam sealer on your luggage, and line each bag with a plastic bag to keep out the wet stuff. The other main disadvantage is that a down bag requires a lot of care when cleaning — again, if used properly, it shouldn't need to be done too often. A liner or underwear worn in the bag will help stave off this event!

Synthetic bags are filled with polyester in a variety of forms, although basically they all use wads of fibres which are stitched into the bags, and which trap the air needed to provide the insulation. Cheaper fillings dictate that more is required to provide a given amount of insulation. The more sophisticated ones have hair-thin fibres with holes running along their length, making the fibres lighter, and able to trap more air. Synthetic fibres are easy to clean, and much more resistant to water, in general only absorbing about 1% of their own weight. Even after being saturated, a synthetic bag will go on insulating where a down bag would be useless.

On the minus side, synthetic bags need to be heavier, because the filling is not so efficient, and they're more bulky. With the exception of fibre-pile, the filling has a shorter life expectancy, particularly if it's left in a compressed state for any length of time. Sophisticated fillings such as Superloft and Quallofil are much softer, but are more expensive than the basic fibres. They're certainly the best compromise between

SLEEPING BAGS

the insulating efficiency of down and the convenience and cheapness of other polyester fibres.

The way the bag is constructed is all-important. Stitched-through quilting is adequate for summer bags, but no use where the weather is cooler. Good down bags have a system of baffles to maintain an even, deep loft, and synthetic bags use a double layer of filling with the stitch lines offset to give better performance.

So how warm is a sleeping bag? Difficult really, because everything is relative to the individual using it. And whilst manufacturers quote the suitability of their bags to various minimum temperatures, or the number of seasons it can be used, it doesn't necessarily mean that everyone will find any particular bag warm enough. Peoples' metabolisms vary, and 'slow burners', or those with poor circulation (perhaps you're not cycling enough) may need a warmer bag. You can, of course, 'uprate' your bag by wearing clothes as well — in practice it's best to restrict this to underwear.

The linings of sleeping bags also have a bearing on the way you prefer to sleep. If you sleep naked, a glazed nylon lining (most commonly found in lightweight bags) will feel cold initially, and then stick to your sweaty little body. Roll over, and the bag will go with you. If you wear nothing in your sleeping bag, you'll find a cotton or poly/cotton lining generally more comfortable. With underwear, the nylon lining assumes the properties of a skating rink, and if your hood isn't done up well, you could wake up the next morning with the back of it on your face. Cotton linings have a slightly higher level of friction with underwear, so the bag will move with you. This question of whether the bag moves with you when you turn over in your sleep isn't just light-hearted amusement. Some bags are designed with less filling in the base than on top, so if the bag turns over with you, you could feel the cold on your back.

Once you've chosen your bag, don't forget something to lie on. The filling compresses beneath you, and provides very little insulation from cold in the ground. A closed-cell foam mat such as the Karrimat is best, if somewhat bulky. For a little extra weight, but less space, you can get a self-inflating foam mattress such as the Thermarest, which provides both insulation and a fair degree of comfort.

Season ratings: Many manufacturers still quote season ratings as a guide to the bag's performance. They should be taken as season ratings in valley conditions. You would need a warmer bag for hill and mountain camps. This is really only a rough guide, but approximate minimum temperatures for each rating are as follows:

1 – 10 degrees C
2 – 0 degrees C
3 – minus 5 degrees C
4 – minus 15 degrees C
5 – below minus 15 degrees C

SLEEPING MATS – *See also Sleeping Bags*

     Luxury for campers always used to be an air-bed. But what sort of luxury is something which is prone to puncturing, and nearly always at the wrong moment? And it's also a fact that an air-bed is not very efficient with your body heat. Your sleeping bag compresses beneath you, so its insulation value is not that high. If the air-bed is laid on cold ground, the air inside it will draw away your body heat in double quick time.

     The answer is an insulating mat. The best ones, made by Karrimor, are lightweight pads of closed-cell foam. They're available in different weights, depending on whether you need an expedition version to cope with extreme cold, or something more moderate for normal camping. Karrimat has almost become a generic term for this type of mat, and although cheaper versions from other manufacturers are available, they're generally of inferior quality, and don't last as long.

     Not only does a closed-cell foam mat provide insulation from cold ground, it's also unaffected by

SNOW BLINDNESS

water. The only drawback is that whilst it is light, it's also relatively bulky. You can also get inflatable mats which do the same job as a Karrimat, but which provide a bit more comfort and support. Basically a piece of foam enclosed by an envelope of coated nylon, you undo a small valve, and the mat inflates itself. Although somewhat heavier than a Karrimat, the good ones are considerably less bulky when packed, and can be folded or rolled to suit your luggage. The very best are the American Thermarest mattresses — but be warned, they're not cheap!

SNOW BLINDNESS

Sounds like the sort of thing only high altitude mountaineers get, but it's possible to get it anywhere where snow and sunshine happen together, although the effects are much more marked with an increase in altitude. It's an extremely painful condition where the eyes become very sore after exposure to intense ultra violet radiation — sunburned retinas, really. It clears up itself if the patient is left in a dark environment, and cold compresses applied over closed eyes can give additional relief.

Because snow reflects UV, it's important to shield your eyes from reflected glare, as well as direct sunlight. Skiers are well catered for with goggles which completely enclose the eyes. Climbers and mountaineers use glacier goggles, which are like sunglasses, but incorporating shields rather like blinkers on each side.

SPACE BLANKET

When these silvery plastic sheets first came out, they were publicised as one of the most significant spin-offs of the space programme. The theory is that the silver surface reflects back 90% of body heat. And that's how they still advertise these things. But in fact, they reflect back 90% of the body heat lost by radiation, which is a mere 10% of your total heat loss.

So what it boils down to is this. Whilst space blankets look very attractive as a lightweight and minimal bulk method of keeping warm, they don't actually do any more than a piece of plain plastic sheeting or coated nylon. In other words, space blankets are a complete waste of money, and what's more, dangerous, because they lull people into a false sense of security!

SPECTACLES

If you're doing a long trip, it's a good idea to carry a spare pair of specs with you, just in case the worst happens. Failing that, a note of your optician's telephone number, or telex, if he has one. That way, you can order a spare pair to be made up. On balance, it's undoubtedly much less trouble to have your spare pair ready, either with you, or at home, if someone there can send them on.

Modern plastic lenses are very lightweight, and can be more comfortable than glass lenses, particularly in hot weather. They need a bit more care when cleaning, and you should never get insect repellent anywhere near them, as the stuff makes the lenses go opaque.

If you're taking a walking/trekking holiday, and you normally wear bi-focals, think again. You need to look at your feet rather more often than you would normally, and it's no good if the lower part of your specs is delivering close-up performance. Get a standard pair of glasses for distance work which will be more suitable for rough country walking.

STOVES

There's nothing more satisfying than a hot cup of tea and a good meal at the end of a long day — if you're out in the wilds, a stove is definitely the travelling person's friend. They come in different shapes and sizes, and it depends largely on the type of use you expect to give it as to which is most appropriate for your needs. First, you have to decide which fuel you want to burn — butane, methylated spirits, paraffin or petrol. You can also get solid fuel burners, but these are inefficient, and not really suited to extended camping trips. The factors to consider here are which fuel you feel safe with, and its availability in the areas in which you're likely to be travelling. Note that when travelling by air, under no circumstances are you allowed to carry any form of camping stove fuel in your baggage, so allow for having to buy your supplies when you arrive.

Each fuel has its advantages and disadvantages. Butane comes in pressurised cartridges, and most stoves are designed to be used with one particular size, although some made for resealing cartridges can take different sizes. Butane is clean, and doesn't need priming, so the stove will light instantly. The disadvantages are that as the fuel uses up, the pressure in the cartridge reduces, and so your cooking times get longer as the gas dwindles. Butane burners are easily affected by the wind, and the liquid gas less willing to vaporise when it's very cold. For lower temperatures, some sizes of cartridge are available with a propane/butane mixture which burns much more readily. Camping Gaz is widely available abroad, although you could find difficulty if you run out somewhere off the beaten track.

Meths is convenient to use. It doesn't need priming, nor does it have to be pressurised. It will bring a kettle to the boil noiselessly, if a little slowly, and leaves no nasty lingering smell if spilt. The stoves designed for burning meths (Trangia, Optimus Trapper) are weatherproof and very stable. On the minus side, meths is rather a sooty burner, and can be difficult to obtain. Whilst you can get it from most hardware stores, there are places where you may either be asked to sign the poison register, or you may not be able to obtain it at all.

Paraffin has to vaporise before it burns efficiently, so the type of stove needed here is pressurised. The fuel itself is reasonably cheap and easy to obtain. It is rather smelly, though, and once spilt, won't evaporate readily. The stove needs a volatile fuel such as petrol or meths to prime it, but once burning, paraffin provides a hot flame.

Petrol is the most widely available, even in the more far-flung reaches of civilisation. It needs more care when handling, as the fumes it gives off are highly volatile. The petrol is burned in a pressurised stove, and is self-priming. Whilst lead-free petrol is by far the best, it's difficult to obtain in this country, and very expensive. Automotive petrol is fine, but never use a higher octane than two-star, and then only with a stove with a built-in jet pricking needle. A stove without this facility will quickly clog up with carbon — trying to strip a stove down for cleaning whilst you're on a camping trip ain't much fun, especially when you're dying for a brew-up!

Both petrol and paraffin need more attention when you first light the stove, as the partially vaporising fuel tends to flare up at the least expected moment. For this reason, and the fact that burning petrol gives off toxic fumes, you should **never** light a stove inside the tent. At the very least, it should be in the open doorway.

STUDENT TRAVEL

If you're in full-time education, it will pay you to get an International Student Identity Card. It can be worth more than its weight in gold, as it qualifies you to a variety of discounts. For travelling in Europe, the Inter Rail Pass is good value — available to anyone under the age of 26. For £139, you get unlimited rail

travel for one month throughout the twenty one
countries participating in the scheme, which is most of
Europe, and Morocco. The pass also allows substantial
discounts on various cross-channel ferries.

SUNBURN — *See also Suncream*

Provided you take adequate precautions, you
shouldn't need to read this! But if the worst happens, a
soothing lotion such as calamine lotion will help put
out some of the fires raging in your skin. Either Aspirin
or anti-histamine tablets will help by reducing the
irritation. Severely burnt skin looks a real mess, puffing
up into blisters. The main concern is to see that
infection doesn't set in.

The sort of person reading this shouldn't be
likely to get into this sort of state, as it more usually
happens to enthusiastic beach sprawlers on the first
day of their holiday. You don't spend your holiday
doing anything so boring, do you? Provided you
behave sensibly, and limit your exposure to short
periods every day, cover up, and use suncream liberally,
you won't get into trouble. If you have access to a
solarium, a few sessions before you travel will help
build up some resistance.

SUNCREAM — *See also Sunburn*

A tube of suncream makes a useful item to pack
in your travel bag, even if you're more likely to be
lashed by cold winds rather than basking in warm
sunshine. It's a good moisturiser which will stop your
skin drying up. If you're fair skinned, you should take
special care when in fierce sun. Sunburn can at least be
extremely painful, and at worst could force you to
change your travel plans entirely.

Suncreams contain ingredients which filter out
UVB rays which cause burning, letting through the less
harmful UVA rays, which promote tanning. They're
sold in varying strengths, identified by their Factor
numbers. The strength of the cream is calculated by
multiplying the Factor number by the normal length of
time you would expect to stay in the sun before
starting to burn. So if you start to burn after ten
minutes exposure, a Factor 6 suncream would give you
an hour. It's best to start off with a fairly high
protection cream at first, and work down to a lower
one once you've started to tan. Once your tan starts to
develop, you achieve a certain built-in protection.

If you're sailing, or walking or climbing in snow,
the reflected glare can be intense, and the risks of
burning much higher. In snow, for example, the

SUN-GLASSES

reflection can be as much as 95%. Banks of cloud can increase the reflection, so you can end up with a lot of UV flying around. Altitude adds to the problem further. After the first 1,000 metres above sea level, UV radiation increases by 100% for every 1,000 metres you climb. So if you're going skiing, you need a suncream with a much higher protection factor than you would have for a summer holiday by the sea.

Use sun block cream, which provides total protection. The professional stuff which comes in small tubes is quite expensive, and once you've smeared the opaque white stuff on your face, you might decide to stay indoors anyway! I've found that Piz Buin, or Coppertone's Factor 15 suncream just as good, and invisible once applied.

The other factor which tends to be ignored is wind-chill. Skiers tend to get this more than most, simply because they're moving faster. The effect is to lower the apparent skin temperature, which can mask the fact that you may be burning. But more of a problem is that the biting cold causes the capillaries in your skin to contract quickly. The tiny blood vessels can burst, causing unsightly perniosis. Water based suncreams can freeze in wind-chill conditions, and make perniosis more likely. Piz Buin do a special cold protection cream, which, like their high altitude glacier cream, is non-water based.

SUN-GLASSES – *See also Hat*

Sun-glasses are an indispensable item of kit for the traveller to bright, sunny places. The glare from a white sandy tropical beach can be intense, as can the sun reflected in snow. In fact, for trips involving more than a few hours in snow, the best type of sun-glasses are of the glacier goggles variety, with side shields, and an optional nose guard. Spectacle wearers may find it easier to have a pair of glasses made with tinted lenses to their prescription, but the most acceptable way these days is to have photochromic lenses, which darken in bright sunlight, and turn clear again once out of the sun.

SUNSTROKE – *See Heat-stroke*

SURVIVAL BAG

If you're out walking in remote country, where the chance of an accident or losing your way might mean an enforced benightment, then a polythene survival bag makes an effective, if somewhat uncomfortable emergency shelter. The only ones which are any good are the 500 gauge bags, usually made from bright orange plastic. Don't buy a space blanket, and don't be seduced by the transparent bags sold in compact pocket size pouches. The plastic is too flimsy for emergency use.

Most people tend to think of a survival bag as something which should be slid into like a sleeping bag. The fallacy here is that such action leads to you lying on the ground full stretch − not good, because there's more of you in contact with the ground, which conducts body heat away at an alarming rate without any insulating mat.

The best way to use a survival bag is to cut the corner off one end of the bag, so you have a hole about one to two inches in diameter. Pull the bag over your head, and sit down on your rucksack. Where possible, choose your position so you're in the lee of a rock, wall, or in a gully. Even inside a plastic bag, you'll be much more comfortable if you can escape the worst ravages of the wind. If you happen to have a longlife candle with you, it will warm up inside your makeshift shelter surprisingly quickly.

T-SHIRTS

T-SHIRTS

The humble T-shirt is a versatile garment for the traveller. Used on its own (although preferably with shorts, trousers or underpants), it's ideal for hot weather. When the mercury starts heading back to base, a T-shirt worn beneath a long sleeved shirt makes a valuable extra layer of insulation. And if you need to wear something in your sleeping bag, it does the job equally well.

TEETH

It pays to check the old gnashers are in good shape before setting off on a trip. After all, you don't want people accusing you of looking down in the mouth, do you? Your travel insurance (you have got it, haven't you?) will cover the expense of any emergency treatment, but it doesn't necessarily follow that the treatment you receive will be up to scratch, particularly if you're travelling in places where dental equipment might not be to the high standard we're used to.

If you're really stuck, and a filling drops out whilst you're in the back of beyond, it is possible to effect a DIY repair which should see you home. Some oil of cloves can be dripped on the spot to kill the pain. Failing that, take a couple of Paracetomols. You can make a temporary filling using some gutta percha (available at chemists). It has to be warmed in hot water, and the softened filler applied to the damaged tooth. Grind the teeth carefully from side to side to press it into place, and continue to take pain killers as needed. Consult a dentist as soon as possible.

TELEPHONING HOME

Over 170 countries subscribe to IDD — International Direct Dialling, so it's usually possible to phone home without too much trouble, and without having to book calls. Each country has an international dialling access code. For example, any international call from the UK is preceded by dialling 010. Next you dial the code of the country you are calling — if you were calling the UK from abroad, it would be 44. Then you dial the area code, but minus the initial 0, followed by the subscriber's number. So, to call Rohan's Milton Keynes headquarters from, say, the United States, you'd dial 011 44 908 618888. Simple, really!

One word of warning. Dialling from your hotel room can seriously damage your bank balance. Most hotels charge an exorbitant mark-up on the actual price of the call, which amounts to daylight robbery. I still wince when I recall the memorable attempt to phone home from a hotel in the Tunisian oasis town of Nefta, on the northern fringes of the Sahara. The call cost me the equivalent of about £5. It lasted roughly thirty seconds, and most galling of all, my wife wasn't in. All I got was my own voice babbling away on the answering machine. Apparently, I was out!

Larger hotels often have a public call box in the lobby, but check first that they can receive incoming calls if you want someone to save you pumping in coins like mad by calling you back. Failing that, your best bet is to drop in to the local post/telecommunications office, where you can usually get a metered call which you can pay for once you've finished.

TENTS

One of my favourite forms of self-catering accommodation. Not on some crowded campsite, though. The lightweight traveller with just his feet, a pair of cycle wheels, or canoe for transport pitches his tent in quiet idyllic settings, far away from the noise and pollution of 'civilisation'.

I smile when I remember the American cycle-tourers I spotted in Norway once. Not only were they loaded to the gills with panniers, bar and saddle bags, as I'd expect most to have. They also had great mounds of shapeless parcels strapped to carriers, cross bars, seat tubes — one even had a small rucksack on his back as well! Heaven knows how they coped with the hills.

Of course, each person has his own requirements for camping, and whilst not everyone will want or be able to pack all his gear into purpose made cycle luggage or rucksacks, it's obviously an advantage to carry equipment of minimal weight, and which can be packed small. In the case of two or more campers, it's also helpful to have gear which will allow the load to be spread evenly.

Tents come in a mind-boggling variety of styles and weights, so you have to decide what sort of use you expect to put your tent to. For two people touring, I wouldn't expect anyone to want or need a tent weighing more than 8 lbs.

How much room do you need? Do you camp solo, or with a partner? If you camp on your own, you have a wide choice of tents, from minuscule bivvy tents and bivvy bags, to solo and lightweight two-man tents. If you camp regularly with a partner, some of the smaller two-man tents may feel a little confined. Provided you get a tent where the various components can be shared out, you can look for one with a little more weight, and room. One or two new designs of tent offer inner and flysheet permanently linked — obviously difficult to share the load here.

TENTS

What sort of weather are you likely to camp in? For (wet) British conditions, a tent with a fully enclosed flysheet is best, offering a porch or 'bell end' in which you can store gear outside the inner tent (wet panniers, muddy shoes etc.), and in which you can cook under shelter. Some American imports have fully or partially enclosed flys without porches, and the cheapo end of the British market has a vast array of models with partial flys. They're generally cotton, and when the ends of the inner get wet, they'll leak as soon as you touch the walls. Then of course, you'll have all your soggy gear in the tent with you, dribbling pools of water onto your sleeping bag and spare clothes.

Even if your camping is confined to the relative shelter of a low-level camp site, it pays to get a tent with fully enclosed fly and porch. For hot countries with insect problems, you'll need a tent with effective insect screening, to provide you with essential ventilation, without the unwelcome attentions of the bug community. Make sure your tent has zipped in insect screening on the outside of the inner doors. If it's on the inside, it defeats the whole object, as you have to unzip the tent to expose the netting.

Beware also of tents which can't be erected flysheet first. Most inner tents have a light proofing to prevent the odd drop of condensation from the fly penetrating, but they won't ward off a cloudburst. If you pitch your flysheet first, everything gets under cover as quickly as possible.

For camping at high level, or on exposed sites, you might also consider the basic design of the tent. Whilst domes and tunnels with flexible hoops offer much greater internal volume for weight, they do with one or two exceptions suffer from a lack of stability once the wind gets up. I've slept in some tents where the ceiling has bounced down onto my nose! The most stable dome tents are geodesic, but these tend to be more specialised, and hence more expensive. A ridge tent with 'A' poles will stand up to all but the strongest winds, and offers an ease of entrance which is lacking in tents with single uprights in the door. Transverse ridge tents generally have lots of storage space, but you might discount them if you don't like the idea of the tent wall sloping sharply over your face.

Cotton tents are the most comfortable — they have no condensation problems, and they're warmer in cold weather. The drawback is that they're heavy compared with nylon, and they add further pounds to your load when they get saturated. An all nylon tent is lighter, and won't soak up water, but because the coated fly can't breath, it's more prone to condensation. The most comfortable compromise, and not much heavier than the all-nylon tent, is one with nylon fly and cotton or poly/cotton inner. Single skin

Gore-Tex tents are light and breathable, but in humid weather, still prone to condensation.

Most tents are supplied in cylindrical stuff sacks, not necessarily the best shape for packing into panniers. Poles can be packed separately, and if they're lightweight flexible poles, the bundle may be small enough to attach to part of the bike frame or rucksack without getting in the way. The rest of the tent can be packed into whatever shape is convenient, with flysheet and inner separate if desired. I usually pack mine in plastic bags.

A piece of polythene cut to the shape of your groundsheet and laid under the tent will reduce wear on the groundsheet, and make packing up easier. Mud is a nuisance to remove from the underside of the groundsheet, and if you use a polythene underlay, the tent will pack up clean (if a little damp) every time.

TENT DESIGNS

Ridge: The traditional ridge tent, whilst not particularly lightweight for the space it offers, is still a favourite with many. Stability and access to the inner tent is improved if it has 'A' poles at both ends.

Transverse ridge: With the ridge running across the sleeping area, this type of design gives you a very spacious 'bell end' on either side of the inner. Good for general backpacking or cycle touring, the large sloping panels tend to catch the wind on exposed pitches, so it's best used in more sheltered places.

Sloping ridge: Another traditional design, brought about originally as a means of making a lighter tent for backpackers by sloping the ridge downwards towards the back. Very stable if pitched tail into the wind.

Single hoop: A lightweight tent held up by a single flexible pole. Sleeping accommodation can be along the ridge, or across, depending on the design. Best pitched with the line of the 'ridge' along the direction of the wind, the guying system is the one factor which can make or break it on exposed pitches.

Tunnel: Tunnel tents generally use two flexible hoops of glass fibre or alloy. Smaller tents emulating a ridge tent usually have a smaller hoop at the tail to give better stability when pitched into the wind. Also available transverse style, with spacious porches for gear storage. Performance tends to be poor in cross winds, and therefore this type of tent is best suited to lowland pitches.

Dome: Generally using three hoops, but sometimes two, all crossing over in the middle rather like a giant brolly. Offers excellent internal space for weight, but performance depends on adequate guying. Because the tent is self supporting, it's particularly well suited

---

to pitching on rough ground, where rocks are more likely to be used to anchor guys than pegs.

Geodesic dome: Same advantages as the dome design, but here, the hoops are offset, not all crossing over at the top. With four and sometimes more poles, geodesic designs can be immensely strong, and are often used by mountaineers in difficult conditions. But because of their specialised nature, geodesics are also the most expensive tents you can get.

Dunnel: As the name suggests, it's a cross between a dome and a tunnel tent, which, because it also uses hoops offset like a geodesic dome, is extremely stable in high winds.

TERRORIST – *See also Hi-jack*

I hope that anyone reading this never falls foul of one. Whatever their cause, and whether you believe it to be right or wrong, the inescapable fact is that if you happen to be in the wrong place at the wrong time, terrorists have little regard for your life beyond its usefulness as a bargaining weapon.

And with the hard line which many western governments have inevitably adopted, it's also a fact that if you fall into the clutches of terrorists, you're on your own. Antagonising them could bring tragic consequences. Those who've come through such dramas have usually done so by trying to establish some form of rapport with their captors.

TETANUS

Cuts or grazes always bring the possibility of tetanus, particularly in the tropics, and where the possibility of immediate medical treatment or adequate cleaning of the wound is unlikely. Immunisation is strongly recommended – the booster gives five years protection.

TICKETS

As a travelling freelance journalist, it's quite often that I'm sent tickets at the very last moment, entailing Red Star or courier deliveries. I thought that 'never ending parcels' were a joke normally confined to tolerant relatives at Christmas. Once, I collected a large padded envelope, about 16 by 13 inches, from my local Red Star depot. Inside was another envelope, 10 by 7 inches, containing yet another envelope, standard letter size. The contents of that one? My railway ticket – a piece of card a little over 2 inches long and 1 inch wide!

But at least I received the all-important ticket in time for my journey. Once you have your tickets, you need to look after them, as you may not be able to get replacements if you lose them. All need not necessarily be lost where you've actually booked your tickets, such as air or ship, where a computer record exists. Keep a separate note of your ticket number — it can help speed things up if it has to be reissued.

Air travellers should check that their return flights don't need to be re-confirmed. If the status, next to the flight details, says OK, you don't need to reconfirm. If it says RQ or SA, you must confirm your seat 72 hours before the flight.

TOILET PAPER

Don't laugh, this is an important subject, and ripe (wipe?) for discussion! Travellers to the more civilised regions of the world may choose to ignore this section, although there are more uses for toilet paper than the obvious. Unexpected spills can be mopped up, spectacles can be polished, noses blown. But it always pays to be prepared, because you might find there isn't any around when you need it the most.

Almost mandatory for third world countries, simply because what's available is more likely to bear a relationship closer to cardboard than the softie stuff you've grown used to. And in the remote areas, you won't find any at all. The locals simply use their left hands and water! If you do go to the toilet out in the wilds, do the decent thing and burn your used paper. It takes longer to decompose than you think.

TORCH

A small torch can be much more useful than just lighting your way to your tent or bunk at night. It could be a life-saver in an emergency situation, where there's a fire in your hotel, your airliner gets into trouble — any situation where normally provided artificial light goes out, just at the time when you want to get out fast. After the Brighton Hotel bombing, Mrs. Thatcher vowed to keep a pocket torch with her at all times in her handbag. In more mundane circumstances, a torch comes into its own once you leave 'civilisation'. Not all hotels and guest houses have a constant supply of electricity! There are several compact torches on the market which are virtually unbreakable, and totally waterproof, whilst providing a powerful beam of light. Mity Lite, Mini Mag Lite and Tekna, all American, are about as good as you can get.

Cycle campers tend to use their battery operated

TRAVELLERS CHEQUES

headlamps for camp use, which obviously saves on weight. For backpacking, and general travelling where you might need some light whilst doing something, the head torch is the perfect answer. Petzl make the best, with the torch unit on the front of the elastic headband, balanced by the battery pack on the back. It's switched on by twisting the lens, and continued twisting focuses the light from a narrow point to a wide beam. Once on, it leaves your hands free to put up tents, read maps, books and timetables, and all the rest!

Make sure you have at least one set of spare batteries with you, and one spare bulb, as you may find them difficult, if not impossible to replace abroad. .

TRAVELLERS CHEQUES – *See also Credit Cards, Money*

Travellers cheques are a fairly safe way of carrying money around. The big advantage is that if you lose them, or they're stolen, you can can get a refund. Sterling travellers cheques are usually accepted in most European countries, the Far East, and Australasia, but they're not welcomed in the States. In fact, US dollar travellers cheques seem a good bet to take anywhere.

The minus side is that you do have to pay for the privilege – first of all when you buy the things, and then there's a commission when you cash them. The banks actually make fortunes from selling travellers cheques each year, because once you've paid for them (usually well in advance of your holiday), it may well be two or three months before they're presented by an overseas bank for payment. And all that time, your money is earning the bank a healthy whack of interest. Most important – keep a separate list of your travellers cheque numbers. You'll need them in the event of your having to report them lost.

TROUSERS

When Levi Strauss made his first pair of jeans from the hard-wearing material used to keep those wild west covered wagons dry, I wonder if he imagined they would still be popular over a hundred years on? Certainly for a large number of uses, jeans make very good casual wear. But for travellers, they have a number of drawbacks. First of all, the material is rather heavy and unforgiving if you happen to be sitting down for a long time. Stretch jeans combat this problem to an extent.

The main drawback is that once wet, whether

'Well, there are down-filled trousers, and down-filled trousers...'

intentionally in the basin, or caught out in a rainstorm, jeans take ages to dry. In fact, they're whole-heartedly discouraged for hill walking, cycling, or any other activity where there's a possibility of mixing rain and wind, because once wet, denim jeans offer no insulation at all. Add to that the fact that they also account for a fair bit of weight and space when packed, and you can see why Rohan Bags are the best-selling modern alternative for travellers.

Made from Airlight polyester/cotton, they're comfortable, and they dry extremely quickly. I've used them on several major long-distance walks in the Highlands, and I wouldn't contemplate using anything else when travelling. There are four zipped pockets, two at the front, and two at the rear, and two unzipped pockets. They're also put together extremely well, with reinforced stitching at all the points of likely strain, and zip fasteners which don't jam or break. They perform well in a wide variety of conditions, and pack into about a third of the space taken by a conventional pair of jeans. Bags are very much the traveller's friends.

TYPHOID

Typhoid is prevalent in places where sanitation and hygiene are dubious. It's caused by contamination of food and water, and produces a prolonged fever which can be fatal if not treated. Vaccination is very effective. If you need this, or a booster, it's best to do it in good time, as in some people (me included) the vaccine produces a reaction not unlike a bad dose of flu, which can lay you up for twenty four hours.

UNDERWEAR

Comfort is the key word here. Don't risk untried new underwear when setting off on a trip. It just might have elastic going all out to pinch you! Some pundits recommend loose boxer shorts for the men, particularly in hot climes. I've never found briefs to be uncomfortable even in savagely hot countries. Cotton ones are best, as their absorbency makes them kinder to you in sticky conditions. Take at least two spare pairs, so you can launder them frequently when necessary. If you're really lazy, I'm told that disposable underwear is quite good, although a little heavy on the wallet/purse.

VISAS – *See appendix for specific requirements*

Information about visas for individual countries becomes obsolete quickly, so you should treat the details about visa requirements contained in the appendix as a rough guide, and check several weeks before you travel as to whether or not you need one. UK Embassy sources have established that 13 million people travel from the UK each year, and at least 4 million of those need visas. Embassies will tell you the score, but don't be tempted to follow any advice about purchasing one at your point of entry, as you may not be able to get one for an extended stay, and language difficulties could add to your problems. Better by far to play safe, and sort it all out before you set off. Note however that a visa doesn't grant you the inalienable right to trek all over your chosen country. You may need additional permits, or you may find some areas restricted, so once again, check before you go!

For a moderate fee, you can take away all the headaches of petty bureaucracy by using a visa service such as that supplied by Thomas Cook, and the Visa Shop. They hold stocks of current Embassy and passport application forms, and have information on vaccinations and medical certificates. They can even supply Visas for countries not represented in the UK, which can save you an awful lot of trouble.

WARMWEAR

The name covers a multitude of sins, from a simple pullover, to all sorts of sophisticated insulated garments for use in extreme cold. The lightweight traveller has to consider what conditions are likely to be encountered. If, for example, you were going hiking in Norway's Jotunheimen Mountains in June, you could expect anything from blazing sunshine to snow. And whatever the weather, you could expect it to be reasonably chilly in the evenings.

The most convenient way to tackle a wide range of temperatures without weighing yourself down, with bulky clothing is to wear several thin garments in layers. In practice, those heavy sweaters and duvets spend most of their time in your luggage, so why lug all that extra weight? If you wear clothing in a series of thin layers, you can put on or take off layers as required, and the clothing you don't use takes up a lot less space in your luggage.

WASH-BAG

It's surprising just how much old junk people take in their wash-bags. A little thought can reduce the weight considerably. For instance, if you're on a relatively short trip, why bother taking a complete bar of soap? Likewise the toothpaste. My preferred method of dealing with this is to rely on the humble 35mm film tub. Its close-fitting lid means you can fill it with toothpaste without any danger of spills, and the tub easily holds enough for two to three weeks, and that's without skimping! It's also possible to slip a cut-down piece of soap into a film tub, although obviously it won't last as long. Most reasonable hotels supply their guests with small bars of soap which are ideal for lightweight wash-bags, many of which come in their own handy plastic boxes.

Liquid shampoo can be decanted into smaller plastic bottles, although, like some brands of toothpaste, you can get certain makes supplied in lightweight plastic tubes. These are preferable in some ways, simply because there's less chance of an almighty mess if the top works loose, and believe me, if it can come undone, it usually does! A bit of foresight when shopping can also help cut the weight of 'undecantable' toiletries like underarm deodorants. The liquid roll-on types often come in heavy glass containers. The stick types are lighter, and some makes are available in small 'sample' sizes, which are ideal for the travelling toilet bag.

Gentlemen who shave might consider using a plastic razor for the duration of their·trip. They weigh virtually nothing. Even if you prefer to use an electric razor, you can get some very light and compact battery razors, notably models made by Sanyo, Remington and Braun.

If you're staying in hotel accommodation all the the time, then you don't need to worry about taking a towel. But elsewhere, it's likely you'll need to carry one, and it's pointless loading yourself down with something big and bulky when what you need is something to dry you off rather than act as an extra garment. I use a kitchen towel, about 16 by 25 inches, and that suits most purposes, including drying off after a bath or shower.

You can get special 'Traveller's Towels' made from ICI Pertex, a close-woven nylon which doesn't so much absorb water, as take it up by capillary action. The one I have measures 4 feet by 1½, and packs up pocket sized. It certainly suffices for drying off face and hands, although I prefer to use the cotton towel for rubbing hair dry. Being synthetic, the Traveller's Towel dries off fairly quickly.

WATER – *See also Sanitation, Food*

Whether you're sitting on a hot, airless bus or train, or you're backpacking across the Sierras, the common factor is that sooner or later you're going to get thirsty. Always take a water flask with you when travelling, and ensure that your water is all right to drink. In fact, it isn't just drinking water you need to be careful about. Even the water you use for cleaning your teeth should be safe. If there's any doubt about the water, whether taken from a tap, or straight from a stream, you should boil it, or sterilise it with a tablet such as those containing either chlorine or iodine. Note that to sterilise water by boiling, you should keep it bubbling for at least five minutes. Boiling kills off all types of disease organisms.

Chlorine tablets like Puritabs kill off bacteria, and despite the anxieties of some, they can dispose of amoebic cysts provided the tablet is left in the water as long as possible before drinking – at least an hour. Iodine tablets, or two to three drops of tincture of iodine in your water will disinfect it, and again should be allowed to stand before drinking.

The other alternative, if it's open to you, is to drink proprietary bottled mineral water. Get a well-known name, and you can be certain it's all right. But be warned, you may get addicted to it. Tap water somehow lacks appeal after you've lived on mineral water for a couple of weeks.

It goes without saying that if you suspect the local water supply, and are either boiling or purifying the tap water, you shouldn't take any drinks with ice made from tap water. Freezing does **not** purify the water! Note also that you should use boiled or purified water for cleaning your teeth. It's just as easy to pick up a bug by swilling dodgy water around your mouth for a few seconds.

When you're working hard, flogging along over rough ground, or in extremely hot weather, you lose body water through sweating. It's your cooling system coming into play, using the principle of evaporation to control your temperature. Because sweat contains electrolytes, mainly sodium, potassium and chloride, past thinking has recommended taking salt tablets in hot weather. In fact, the concentration of electrolytes in sweat is much lower than it is in the blood. When you sweat, fluid is lost from the body, increasing the concentration of electrolytes in the blood. So it's useless to add more — what you need to do is replace the lost fluid. But low concentrations of salt and glucose in the water helps the body absorb the fluid more readily, the same reason why it's used for re-hydration during a bout of diarrhoea.

When it comes to carrying your water supplies around with you, don't be tempted to get the army style canteen. The round shape isn't practical, and the top can sometimes leak. The best bottles for carrying water are the Swiss made Sigg bottles — aluminium, and with a screw top incorporating a neoprene rubber seal. My two bottles are ten years old, smothered in dents, and still perfectly serviceable. No other bottle would have survived the treatment they've soaked up. (Note: Sigg make plain aluminium bottles intended for fuel, also excellent. They shouldn't be used for drinking water, though, as they tend to impart a metallic taste to the water. Sigg water bottles are coloured red or blue, and are lacquered inside to prevent taste transfer.)

WATERPROOFS

Keeping dry whenever you possibly can makes sense, as anyone can discover if they find themselves tramping for hours through driving rain. Even if you aren't expecting to do any wilderness walking, back country backpacking or mountain hopping, a jacket and trousers in 100% waterproof material will serve you well.

Styles vary enormously — the thing which determines price more than anything is the fabric. Although you can pick up silicone proofed nylon rainwear dirt cheap from department stores, they don't hold off more than light showers, so to all intents and purposes, they're useless. Polyurethane coated nylon is the cheapest reliable fabric used for waterproofs. Its disadvantage, as indeed is with the more hard-wearing neoprene coated nylon, is that because it's impervious to moisture vapour, it allows an uncomfortable build-up of condensation. If the weather is cold, and you exert yourself, the effect will be more pronounced.

The last few years have seen the emergence of several different fabrics which alleviate the problem by transmitting moisture vapour through the material, whilst still remaining waterproof. Gore-Tex is the most well-known, and widely considered the best, although competing materials appearing on the market could sway the balance. Gore-Tex consists of an expanded PTFE membrane, with billions of tiny pores, large enough to permit the passage of water vapour molecules, but not large enough for liquid water molecules to penetrate. The membrane itself is quite weak, and so has to be laminated to other fabrics in order to give it the strength for use in waterproof garments.

The better waterproof garments have tape sealed seams. They used to be doped with contact adhesive, but after a while, the doping would dry out and peel off. Modern seam-sealing uses tape applied by a machine which blows a jet of hot air to melt the pre-glued surface, and then presses it onto the fabric. The result is a much more lasting seal which keeps the wet out.

Whichever price bracket you aim for, and whichever material, consider what your most likely uses will be for your rainwear. The heavy-duty mountain climbing and walking wet weather suits will be over-specified for you if all you want is something to keep the rain off whilst you wait at the bus stop. Moisture vapour permeable materials are available in a variety of laminates and coatings, so your jacket and trousers don't want to be light and flimsy if you plan on backpacking a great deal – simply because the lighter weight materials can't take much hard wearing.

WESTERN VALUES – *See also Attitude*

Of all the travellers most likely to penetrate the true culture of a country, it's those that travel light, and who don't spend every night in the Hiltons and Sheratons of this world. It's only once you get away from the big cities that the people show their true colours.

I suppose drawing comparisons is natural enough. You might comment on the price of a piece of cheese in a Dutch supermarket, or wonder at the massive overhanging roof of a Swiss chalet. But further afield, the so-called western way of life is either alien,

WHISTLE

or merely aspired to, and sometimes practised in ways which might seem strange or even comical to the outsider.

But the biggest mistake any traveller can make is not to accept everything he sees or experiences at face value. It's all too easy to look down on people because they don't meet your expectation of western standards. Just because all our sewage is piped away and treated doesn't mean that people who use open sewers are any less fastidious than you. Indeed, there are many cultures where washing is a frequent ritual task. It may be that you're the smelly one!

Neither should you turn your nose up, or feel sorry for people living on a staple diet of what you might think are uninteresting vegetables. They aren't the ones dying of heart disease and other ailments brought on by a lifetime of eating over-refined food with dubious chemical additives. Things aren't better, or worse. Just different. Once you've accepted that, you'll find it easier to distinguish between those living simply, and those with real poverty.

If you feel the need to draw comparisons, don't forget that when it comes to civilisation, in terms of architecture, social structure, writing and the arts, you're the newcomer. South America, China, India, Persia, Italy and Egypt all had dazzling civilisations when the Ancient Brits were still wandering around in animal skins, and living in mud huts!

You might think your own standards ought to be universal, but they're not. Despite the insidious creeping influence of the west, the rest of the world is a lot richer for keeping its individuality. And that, surely, is the reason why we travel.

WHISTLE

Out in wild country, a whistle is a useful means of attracting attention in an emergency. A plastic Perry whistle weighs next to nothing, and produces a suitably ear-splitting shriek when called upon. The international distress signal is six blasts of the whistle, followed by a pause of one minute, and then repeated. The reply to the distress signal is three blasts, followed by a minute's pause, and then repeated. Only to be used at railway stations in moments of extreme anguish.

WIND-CHILL

For any given air temperature, the cooling effect becomes more marked with corresponding increases in wind speed. When it's blazing hot, a cooling breeze

might be most welcome, but at lower temperatures, even a moderate wind can have a dramatic effect on how cold you feel. The wind-chill factor charts below give the equivalent temperatures on exposed flesh, showing how cold it would have to be if there were no wind at all to provide the same cooling effect.

Wind Speed mph	Air Temperature, degrees Fahrenheit												
	35	30	25	20	15	10	5	0	-5	-10	-15	-20	-25
10	21	16	9	2	-2	-9	-15	-22	-27	-31	-38	-45	-52
15	16	11	1	-6	-11	-18	-25	-33	-40	-45	-51	-60	-65
20	12	3	-4	-9	-17	-24	-32	-40	-46	-52	-60	-68	-76
25	7	0	-7	-15	-22	-29	-37	-45	-52	-58	-67	-75	-83
30	5	-2	-11	-18	-26	-33	-41	-49	-56	-63	-70	-78	-87
35	3	-4	-13	-20	-27	-35	-43	-52	-60	-67	-72	-83	-90
40	1	-4	-15	-22	-29	-36	-45	-54	-62	-69	-76	-87	-94

Wind Speed kph	Air Temperature, degrees Celsius												
	8	4	0	-4	-8	-12	-16	-20	-24	-28	-32	-36	
10	5	0	-4	-8	-13	-17	-22	-26	-31	-35	-40	-44	
20	0	-5	-10	-15	-21	-26	-31	-36	-42	-47	-52	-57	
30	-3	-8	-14	-20	-25	-31	-37	-43	-48	-54	-60	-65	
40	-5	-11	-17	-23	-29	-35	-41	-47	-53	-59	-65	-71	
50	-6	-12	-18	-25	-31	-37	-43	-49	-56	-62	-68	-74	
60	-7	-13	-19	-26	-32	-39	-45	-51	-58	-64	-70	-77	
70	-7	-14	-20	-27	-33	-40	-46	-52	-59	-65	-72	-78	

WOMEN TRAVELLERS

It's rather sad that only up until recently, in most parts of the world, western women who travelled alone were regarded as eccentric, promiscuous, or both. But even with today's more liberal attitudes, you don't have to travel as far as the third world to discover the still entrenched sexual prejudices. Lone women travellers must be prepared to face harassment from those that think it improper of them not to be trailing six paces behind their husbands, and harassment from those whose sole purpose it is to take advantage of the lack of protective males.

Mind you, don't automatically assume safety if you do happen to be travelling with a male. Some perverts take pleasure in assaulting a girl, and making her partner watch! Neither should you assume that the man being nice to you is safe just because he has his wife with him. There are kinky women around too. Be careful what you eat or drink when in the company of others. Many girls in strange cities have never been seen again except in drug clinics, and the sort of films Barry Norman doesn't review.

But on the whole, harassment is usually intended as just a bit of fun on the part of the harasser. Rape is still comparatively rare, and not condoned by any society. And even if it does come to the worst possible eventuality, unless you're expert in the ways of self-defence, or you believe that rape really is a fate worse than death, your best hope is to offer no resistance. The experience will be unpleasant, it may scar you mentally for life, but at least you'll still be alive! By co-operating, you might win yourself some valuable few seconds — possibly to be able to kick him where it hurts most when his trousers are down. It's very difficult to run like that!

Having painted the darkest picture, one should point out that the vast majority of ladies travelling alone or with other female companions have no problems at all, other than the more innocent troubles which most can handle.

Experienced women travellers tell me that there are two ways of dealing with awkward and unwelcome male attentions where the man is either showing off in front of his friends, or trying to be an amateur Romeo rather than the Yorkshire Ripper. The first is to play the fierce English school ma'am. You do need the right sort of character (and build) to carry it off, but done at maximum volume, success is usually marked by embarassing your adversary into a cowering timid jelly. Another interesting variation is to learn the local language for 'naff off, you creep', and even 'help, rape!'

The other is to employ your feminine wiles to

your advantage. Smile disarmingly, and the chances are your harasser will become putty in your hands. Most cases of sexual harassment occur when groups of men or youths are trying to show off by provoking a reaction from you. By turning on a smile and playing the little girl lost, you rob them of their moment of fun. In fact, they may well offer you some genuine assistance!

Dress modestly. Anything exposing too much flesh, or showing too much of what one might call shape, is likely to be considered either a come-on, or insulting, depending on which part of the world you're in.

X-RAY

X-RAY

It's part and parcel of the ever-tightening vigilance against terrorists that your hand baggage will have to be passed through an X-Ray machine on your way through airport security. In fact, with some of the airlines more at risk than others operating their own security checks as well, your hand luggage may well go through an X-Ray more than once before you actually board your aircraft. This doesn't present any particular problems other than for photographers.

The big international airports generally use the latest low dosage machines, and it's likely that they will even display notices informing you that they don't harm films up to 1000 ASA. (The up to date standard for film speeds is ISO, but the values are the same.) That's perfectly true, at least for up to two or three passes through such machines. X-Rays, like light, have a cumulative effect on film emulsion. If you happen to do a lot of hopping about by air, and your film has been X-Rayed half a dozen times, there's no way that it will escape without some degree of fogging.

At the lowest end of damage, your film might just come out with reduced definition and contrast. At the very worst, your film could be completely fogged, with the shadow of the spool in the cassette repeating itself all the way down the film. The faster the film speed (the higher the ISO number), the more sensitive the film to light **and** X-Rays.

In many airports, the people operating these machines have been programmed to tell you that your film won't be harmed by X-Rays, and if you're only likely to pass through a couple of times, it would probably pay not to argue. But if you're likely to pass through a number of airports before your film is finally developed, it can pay to ask very politely for a hand search. Keep your film separate, in a plastic bag, and never leave the film in a camera, as they will rightly insist on putting that through. Busy periods may mean you'll be unlucky, but it's always worth asking. If the situation gets desperate, and you can't possibly afford to let your films go through, then you'd better have time to spare. People who make a fuss tend to get frisked for the hell of it.

British airports are no problem. They'll be pleased to hand search anything on request. I discovered that Zürich and Schiphol airports won't countenance it even if you go down on hands and knees. Sometimes you can get away with carrying small amounts of film in your pockets, although sensitive metal detectors can be set off by it, and of course, your 'frisker' may then decide to relieve you of your burden and put it through the machine. But quite often, you can get away with it. Elsewhere, I've 'smuggled' film through the metal detector, and played the innocent when frisked. It might seem a lot of trouble to go to, but if your pictures are priceless, it's worth the effort to protect them.

At less well-equipped airports, the X-Ray machines may be of the older variety, where instead of passing luggage along a conveyor belt, it's placed into the machine, and a sliding door drawn over the top. These are most decidedly **not** safe for films, as the dosage is considerably higher. On the plus side, the metal detectors may not be so brilliant, and you may get away with walking through with all your films distributed about your pockets.

You can buy lead-lined film bags which are supposed to stop X-Rays getting through to your films. The theory is sound enough, provided the X-Ray operator recognises the shadow he sees on the screen. Don't discount the possibility that he'll give your bag a bigger dose so he **can** see what's inside, and in the process expose your precious films to what the lead-lined bag was supposed to avoid!

You might find it worth trying another ploy. Now that 1600 ISO films (Fuji) are available, why not keep a couple of rolls with you. You can produce them at the security check, and rightly point out that as their machine is only rated safe up to 1000, they must give you a hand search!

YELLOW FEVER

A virus infection spread by mosquitoes, but not the same family as those which spread malaria. Affected areas of the world are Central Africa and Central America. Vaccination is mandatory for visits to countries in these areas, and for many others further afield if you have transited an affected area in the six days prior to your arrival. Immunity takes ten days to develop after vaccination, from which point your ten year certificate of cover will be valid. The certificate must be produced for immigration officials where required, or you'll be refused entry.

YOUTH HOSTELS — *See appendix for address of YHA*

Youth Hostels are a great introduction to travel for the young, and even for the not so young. They represent budget accommodation coupled with the opportunity of meeting an interesting cross-section of people. It's not like a hotel, of course. And whilst some new hostels are going for smaller rooms, the norm is still fairly large, segregated dormitory sleeping arrangements. You might get a choice of meals if you're lucky.

Whatever's on offer will be good basic fare, and you'll be expected to complete some chore, such as sweeping the dining room floor before you depart in the morning. Bedding is generally supplied. All you need to supply is your own sheet sleeping bag, so without a sleeping bag, your luggage can be kept down to a minimum. There's no fixed upper age limit for membership of the Youth Hostels Association, although in some countries, where there's pressure on space in hostels, you may find preference being given to younger people.

ZOOM

This is, after all, an A to Z, so it would be unfitting to end on the letter Y. Zoom is something all the preceding advice will enable you to do when you travel. But don't feel this new-found knowledge obliges you in any way to alter your pace. You still need to hang around long enough to see the horizons which travelling is supposed to broaden!

'There goes a real lightweight traveller...'

APPENDICES

AIRPORTS

AIRPORTS – Countries A to Z Worldwide

Abu Dhabi	AUH	Abu Dhabi International
Adelaide	ADL	Adelaide
Algiers	ALG	Houari Boumediene
Amsterdam	AMS	Schiphol International
Athens	ATH	Hellinikon
Atlanta	ATL	William B. Hartsfield
Auckland	AKL	Mangere International
Bahrain	BAH	Muharraq
Bangkok	BKK	International
Barbados	BGI	Grantley Adams
Beijing	PEK	Capital
Beirut	BEY	International
Belgrade	BEG	Belgrade
Berlin, West	BER	Tegel
Bermuda	BDA	Kindley Field
Bombay	BOM	Bombay
Boston	BOS	Logan International
Brisbane	BNE	Brisbane International
Brussels	BRU	National
Buenos Aires	BUE	Ezeiza, Aeroparque Jorge, Newbury
Cairo	CAI	International
Calcutta	CCU	Calcutta
Canberra	CBR	Canberra
Capetown	CPT	D. F. Malan
Casablanca	CAS	Mohamed V
Chicago	CHI	O'Hare International, Midway, Meigs Field
Cleveland	CLE	Cleveland Hopkins
Colombo	CMB	Katunayake International
Copenhagen	CPH	Kastrup
Dallas/Fort Worth	DFW	Regional, Love Field
Dar-es-Salaam	DAR	International
Delhi	DEL	Indira Ghandi International
Denver	DEN	Stapleton International
Detroit	DTT	Metropolitan, City Airport
Djibouti	JIB	Djibouti
Dubai	DXB	Dubai
Dublin	DUB	International
Durban	DUR	Louis Botha
Dusseldorf	DUS	Dusseldorf
Edmonton	YEG	International, Municipal Airport
Frankfurt	FRA	Frankfurt International
Freetown	FNA	Lungi International, Hastings
Geneva	GVA	Geneva
Halifax	YHZ	International
Hamburg	HAM	Fuhlsbuttel
Harare	HRE	Harare
Helsinki	HEL	Helsinki-Vantaa
Honolulu	HNL	International
Hong Kong	HKG	Kai Tak
Houston	HOU	Intercontinental, Hobby Airport
Istanbul	IST	Yesilkov
Jeddah	JED	King Abdulaziz International
Jerusalem	JRS	Atarot
Johannesburg	JNB	Jan Smuts
Kansas City	MKC	International
Karachi	KHI	Civil
Kuala Lumpur	KUL	Subang International

AIRPORTS

Kuwait	KWI	International
Las Vegas	LAS	McCarran International
Lisbon	LIS	Lisbon
London Gatwick	LGW	Gatwick
London Heathrow	LHR	Heathrow
London Stansted	LST	Stansted
Los Angeles	LAX	International, Burbank
Madrid	MAD	Barajas
Malta, Valetta	MLA	Luga
Marseille	MRS	Marignana
Melbourne	MEL	Tullamarine
Memphis	MEM	International
Mexico City	MEX	Benito Juarez International
Miami	MIA	International
Milan	MIL	F. Forlanini-Linate
Minneapolis/St. Paul	MSP	Minneapolis/St. Paul International
Montreal	YUL	Dorval, Mirabel
Moscow	MOW	Sheremetyevo International
Nairobi	NBO	Jomo Kenyatta, Wilson
Nassau	NAS	International
New Orleans	MSY	International
New York	NYC	
John F. Kennedy	JFK	John F. Kennedy
La Guardia	LGA	La Guardia
Newark, N.J.	EWR	Newark
Nice	NCE	Cote d'Azur
Osaka	OSA	International
Oslo	OSL	Gardermoen
Ottowa	YOW	Uplands International
Panama City	PTY	Omar Torrijos Herrera
Paris	PAR	
Charles de Gaulle	CDG	Charles de Gaulle
Orly	ORY	Orly
Perth	PER	Perth
Philadelphia	PHL	International, North Philadelphia
Pittsburgh	PIT	Greater Pittsburgh
Prague	PRG	Ruzyné
Quebec	YQB	Quebec
Reykjavik	REY	Keflavik
Riyadh	RUH	King Khaled International
Rio de Janeiro	RIO	International, Santos Dumont
Rome	ROM	Leonardo da Vinci, Fiumicino
Salt Lake City	SLC	International
San Diego	SAN	Lindbergh International
San Francisco	SFO	International
Seattle	SEA	Seattle-Tacoma International
Singapore	SIN	Changi, Seletar
St. Louis	STL	Lambert International
Stockholm	STO	Arlanda
Sydney	SYD	Kingsford Smith
Tangier	TNG	Boukhalef Souahel
Tel Aviv	TLV	Ben Gurion International
Tokyo	TYO	Haneda, Narita
Toronto	YYZ	Lester B. Pearson International
Vancouver	YVR	International
Vienna	VIE	Schwechat
Washington D.C.	WAS	Dulles International, National
Wellington	WLG	International
Winnipeg	YWG	International
Zurich	ZRH	Zurich

CLOTHING LIST

Quite obviously, it's difficult to cover all possibilities, but the following makes a useful basic kit which you should find sufficient for most conditions from as hot as it might ever get, down to around freezing.

Shirts, lightweight – 2

Preferably long sleeved, so you can cover up against insects, and the sun when it's too fierce.

T-Shirts – 2

Soft 'wicking' fabrics such as Dunova or polypropylene are ideal if you're doing something reasonably energetic, and working up a sweat. Also very warm when used as underwear.

If you're in a hot climate, and not exerting yourself so much, a loose fitting polycotton T-Shirt will allow the air to circulate. Alternatively, roll up the sleeves of your long sleeved shirt.

Windshirt – 1

Lightweight, close-woven polycotton, it does just as the name suggests. Very effective in cool conditions with a thin warm layer beneath.

Midwear

A woollen jumper is nice and warm, but takes ages to dry if you wash it. Synthetic alternatives include fibre pile, fleece, and jackets or sweaters made with a thin layer of insulating wadding such as Quallofil or Isodry. The insulating properties of your warm layer are greatly enhanced by the addition of a windproof layer.

Trousers – 1 or 2 pairs

Lightweight, polycotton, with zipped pockets. Comfortable over a wide variety of temperatures, and quick drying if they get wet.

Skirt – 1

Ladies might wish to substitute one pair of trousers for this, particularly for countries where they might cause offence. If you wear a skirt in those circumstances, go for one which is reasonably voluminous, and fairly long.

Shorts – 1

NOT running shorts for sightseeing! Most useful with a few pockets. Polycotton material same as trousers and windshirt, dries out very quickly after washing.

Waterproofs

Wild country travellers will need a full set, jacket and trousers. Modern breathable fabrics give added versatility by doubling as comfortable windproof clothing even when it isn't raining. Also improves the insulation of warm layers beneath. Travellers not likely to be exposed to foul weather for hours on end needn't bother with waterproof trousers.

Thermal underwear – 1 set

Available in a wide variety of fabrics – natural wool or silk, or synthetics such as Dunova or Capilene. Used as underwear and pyjamas.

Hat
Wide brimmed for sunny conditions, or woolly hat or balaclava for cold.

Socks — 2 pairs
Wash and interchange regularly. Loopstitch socks for walking.

Underwear — 2 pairs
Same as socks. Wash one, wear the other.

Bathing costume
Gents keen on saving every ounce might prefer to let their shorts double for this. Or if propriety allows, why not do without the cozzie altogether?

CONVERSION CHARTS

LENGTH *(Conversion Charts)*

Inches	Centimetres	Centimetres	Inches
1	2.54	1	0.394
2	5.08	2	0.787
3	7.62	3	1.181
4	10.16	4	1.575
5	12.70	5	1.969
6	15.24	6	2.362
7	17.78	7	2.756
8	20.32	8	3.150
9	22.86	9	3.543
10	25.40	10	3.937
20	50.80	20	7.874
30	76.20	30	11.811
40	101.60	40	15.748
50	127.00	50	19.685
60	152.40	60	23.622
70	177.80	70	27.559
80	203.20	80	31.496
90	228.60	90	35.433
100	254.00	100	39.370

Miles	Kilometres	Kilometres	Miles
1	1.609	1	0.621
2	3.219	2	1.243
3	4.828	3	1.864
4	6.437	4	2.485
5	8.047	5	3.107
6	9.656	6	3.728
7	11.265	7	4.350
8	12.875	8	4.971
9	14.484	9	5.592
10	16.093	10	6.214
20	32.187	20	12.427
30	48.280	30	18.641
40	64.374	40	24.855
50	80.467	50	31.069
60	96.561	60	37.282
70	112.654	70	43.496
80	128.748	80	49.710
90	144.841	90	55.923
100	160.934	100	62.137

1 inch = 2.54 centimetres
1 foot = 0.3048 metres
1 yard = 0.9144 metres
1 mile = 1.6093 kilometres

1 millimetre = 0.0394 inches
1 centimetre = 0.3937 inches
1 metre = 1.0936 yards
1 kilometre = 0.6214 miles

CONVERSION CHARTS

TEMPERATURE *(Conversion Charts)*

Celsius	Fahrenheit	Fahrenheit	Celsius
-20	-4	-5	-20
-15	5	0	-18
-10	14	10	-12
-5	23	20	-7
0	32	30	-1
5	41	40	4
10	50	50	10
15	59	60	15
20	68	70	21
25	77	80	27
30	86	90	32
35	95	100	38
40	104		
45	113		

Celsius to Fahrenheit — Multiply degrees Celsius by 9/5, and add 32

Fahrenheit to Celsius — Subtract 32 from degrees Fahrenheit, and multiply by 5/9

VOLUME *(Conversion Charts)*

Gallons	Litres	Litres	Gallons
1	4.546	1	0.220
2	9.092	2	0.440
3	13.638	3	0.660
4	18.184	4	0.880
5	22.730	5	1.100
6	27.276	6	1.320
7	31.822	7	1.540
8	36.368	8	1.760
9	40.914	9	1.980
10	45.460	10	2.200
20	90.919	20	4.399
30	136.379	30	6.599
40	181.839	40	8.799
50	227.298	50	10.998
60	272.758	60	13.198
70	318.217	70	15.398
80	363.677	80	17.598
90	409.137	90	19.797
100	454.596	100	21.997

1 cu. inch = 16.387 cu. centimetres
1 cu. foot = 0.0283 cu. metres
1 pint = 0.5683 litres
1 gallon = 4.5464 litres

1 cu. centimetre = 0.0610 cu. inches
1 cu. decimetre = 0.0353 cu. feet
1 litre = 1.7600 pints
1 litre = 0.2200 gallons

CONVERSION CHARTS

WEIGHT *(Conversion Charts)*

Pounds	Kilograms	Kilograms	Pounds
1	0.454	1	2.205
2	0.907	2	4.409
3	1.361	3	6.614
4	1.814	4	8.819
5	2.268	5	11.023
6	2.722	6	13.228
7	3.175	7	15.432
8	3.629	8	17.637
9	4.082	9	19.842
10	4.536	10	22.046
20	9.072	20	44.092
30	13.608	30	66.139
40	18.144	40	88.185
50	22.680	50	110.231
60	27.216	60	132.277
70	31.752	70	154.324
80	36.287	80	176.370
90	40.823	90	198.416
100	45.359	100	220.462

1 ounce = 28.35 grams
1 pound = 0.4536 kilograms
1 ton   = 1.011 tonne

1 gram   = 0.0353 ounces
1 kilogram = 2.2046 pounds
1 tonne   = 0.9842 tons

NATIONAL TOURIST OFFICES

ANTIGUA and BARBUDA – 15 Thayer Street, London, W1M 5LD. Tel: 01 486 7073

AUSTRALIA – 4th Floor, Heathcote House, 20 Savile Row, London, W1X 1AE. Tel: 01 434 4372

AUSTRIA – 30 St. George Street, London, W1R 0AL. Tel: 01 629 0461

BAHAMAS – 10 Chesterfield Street, London, W1X 8AH. Tel: 01 629 5238, 491 4800

BARBADOS – 263 Tottenham Court Road, London, W1. Tel: 01 636 0090

BELGIUM – 38 Dover Street, London, W1X 3RB. Tel: 01 499 5379

BERMUDA – 6 Burnsall Street, London, SW3 3ST. Tel: 01 734 8813

BRITISH VIRGIN ISLANDS – 26 Hockerill Street, Bishop's Stortford, Hertfordshire. Tel: 0279 54969

BULGARIA – 18 Princes Street, London, W1R 7RE. Tel: 01 499 6988

CANADA – Canada House, Trafalgar Square, London, SW14 5BJ. Tel: 01 629 9492

CAYMAN ISLANDS – Hambleton House, 17b Curzon Street, London, W1Y 7FE. Tel: 01 491 7756, 493 5161

CYPRUS – 213 Regent Street, London, W1R 8DA. Tel: 01 734 9822/2593

CZECHOSLAVAKIA – Cedok, 17-18 Old Bond Street, London, W1X 4RB. Tel: 01 629 6058

DENMARK – 169-173 Regent Street, London, W1R 8PY. Tel: 01 734 2637/8

FALKLAND ISLANDS – 294 Tadcaster Road, York, YO2 2ET. Tel: 0904 702059

FIJI – Suite 433, High Holborn, London, WC1V 6BR.

FINLAND – 66 Haymarket, London, SW1Y 4RF. Tel: 01 839 4048

FRANCE – 178 Piccadilly, London, W1V 0AL. Tel: 01 499 6911

EAST GERMANY – Berolina Travel Ltd., 22 Conduit Street, London, W1R 9TB. Tel: 01 629 1664

WEST GERMANY – 61 Conduit Street, London, W1R 0EN. Tel: 01 734 5853

GIBRALTAR – Arundel Great Court, 179 Strand, London, WC2R 1EH. Tel: 01 836 0777

GREECE – 195-197 Regent Street, London, W1R 8DL. Tel: 01 734 5997

HAWAII – 16 Bedford Square, London, WC1B 3JA. Tel: 01 580 4392

HONG KONG – 125 Pall Mall, London, SW1Y 5EA. Tel: 01 930 4775

HUNGARY – 6 Conduit Street, London, W1. Tel: 01 493 0263

INDIA – 7 Cork Street, London, W1X 2AB. Tel: 01 437 3677/8

INDONESIA – 35 Duke Street, London, W1. Tel: 01 935 5036

IRELAND – 150-151 New Bond Street, London, W1Y 0AQ. Tel: 01 493 3201

ISRAEL – 18 Great Marlborough Street, London, W1V 1AF. Tel: 01 434 3651

ITALY – 1 Princes Street, London, W1R 8AY. Tel: 01 408 1254

JAMAICA – 63 St. James's Street, London, SW1A 1LY. Tel: 01 499 1707/8, 493 3647

JAPAN – 167 Regent Street, London, W1R 7FD. Tel: 01 734 9638

NATIONAL TOURIST OFFICES

KENYA – 45 Portland Place, London, W1N 4AS. Tel: 01 636 2371

KOREA – Vogue House, 1 Hanover Square, London, W1R 9RD. Tel: 01 408 1591

LUXEMBOURG – 36-37 Piccadilly, London, W1. Tel: 01 434 2800

MALAYSIA – 57 Trafalgar Square, London, WC2N 5DU. Tel: 01 930 7932

MALTA – 207 College House, Wrights Lane, London, W8. Tel: 01 938 2668

MEXICO – 7 Cork Street, London, W1X. Tel: 01 734 1058/59

MONACO – 34 Sackville Street, London, W1. Tel: 01 437 3660

MOROCCO – 174 Regent Street, London, W1R 6HB. Tel: 01 437 0073

NETHERLANDS – 25/28 Buckingham Gate, London, SW1E 6LD. Tel: 01 630 0451

NEW ZEALAND – New Zealand House, Haymarket, London, SW1Y 4TQ. Tel: 01 930 8422

NORWAY – 20 Pall Mall, London, SE1Y 5NE. Tel: 01 839 6255

PAKISTAN – Suite 433, High Holborn House, 52-54 High Holborn, London, WC1V 6RL. Tel: 01 242 3131

PERU – 10 Grosvenor Gardens, 1st Floor, London, SW1 0BD. Tel: 01 730 7122

POLAND – Polorbis, 82 Mortimer Street, London, W1N 7DE. Tel: 01 580 8028, 636 2217

PORTUGAL – 1-5 New Bond Street, London, W1Y 0NP. Tel: 01 493 3873

ROMANIA – 77-81 Gloucester Place, London, W1. Tel: 01 935 8590

SIERRA LEONE – 40-41 Conduit Street, London, W1R 9FB. Tel: 01 491 3291

SINGAPORE – Carrington House, 126-130 Regent Street, London, W1R 5FE. Tel: 01 439 8111

SOUTH AFRICA – Regency House, 1-4 Warwick Street, London, W1R 5WB. Tel: 01 439 9661

SPAIN – 57-58 St. James's Street, London, SW1A 1LD. Tel: 01 499 1243

SRI LANKA – Quadrant House, 4 Tavistock Place, London, WC1H 9RA. Tel: 01 278 0639

SWEDEN – 3 Cork Street, London, W1X 1HA. Tel: 01 437 5816

SWITZERLAND – Swiss Centre, New Coventry Street, London, W1V 8EE. Tel: 01 734 1921

THAILAND – 9 Stafford Street, London, W1X 3FE. Tel: 01 499 7679

TUNISIA – 33 Dover Street, London, W1. Tel: 01 629 0858

TURKEY – 170-173 Piccadilly, 1st Floor, London, W1V 9DD. Tel: 01 734 8681/2

UNITED STATES VIRGIN ISLANDS – 16 Bedford Square, London, WC1B 3JA. Tel: 01 637 8481/2

USA – 22 Sackville Street, London, W1X 2EA. Tel: 01 437 0555

USSR – Intourist, 292 Regent Street, London, W1R 6QL. Tel: 01 631 1252

YUGOSLAVIA – 143 Regent Street, London, W1R 8AE. Tel: 01 734 3969

ZAMBIA – 2 Palace Gate, Kensington, London, W8 5NG. Tel: 01 589 6343

ZIMBABWE – Colette House, 52-55 Piccadilly, London, W1V 9AA. Tel: 01 629 3955

SHORT WAVE RADIO FREQUENCIES

SHORT WAVE RADIO FREQUENCIES

Listed here are some of the leading international broadcasting organisations providing English language broadcasts on short wave. Note that short wave reception is affected by atmospheric conditions, sunspots, and other disturbances. The frequencies shown are all in KHz.

BBC World Service

North America: *5975, 6120, 6175, 6195, 7325, 9510, 9515, 9740, 9915, 11750, 11775, 15070, 15215, 15260, 17790, 21550*
Europe: *648, 810, 1296, 3955, 3990, 5975, 6010, 6015, 6050, 6180, 6195, 7120, 7150, 7185, 7325, 9410, 9580, 9660, 9750, 9760, 11750, 11760, 11955, 12095, 15070, 17705, 17790, 21470, 21550, 21710*
Middle East: *639, 702, 720, 1323, 1413, 6050, 7160, 7325, 9410, 11740, 11760, 11955, 12095, 15070, 15380, 15420, 17790, 21710*
Africa: *1413, 5975, 6005, 6180, 6190, 7140, 7160, 7185, 7325, 9410, 9515, 9600, 9715, 11745, 11750, 11830, 11860, 11955, 12095, 15070, 15400, 15420, 15445, 17705, 17740, 17790, 17880, 17885, 18080, 21470, 21640, 21660, 21710, 25650*
South America: *5975, 6005, 6120, 6175, 7325, 9515, 9915, 11750, 15260*
Australia and New Zealand: *5975, 6195, 7145, 7150, 7325, 9410, 9510, 9570, 9640, 9740, 11750, 11775, 11955, 15070, 15310, 21550*
South Asia: *1413, 5965, 6195, 7135, 7160, 9410, 9580, 9740, 11750, 11760, 11955, 15070, 15310, 15380, 17790, 21550, 21710*
East and South East Asia: *3915, 6195, 7120, 9570, 9740, 11750, 11955, 15280, 15310, 15435, 17880, 21550*

Voice of America

Europe: *792, 1197, 3980, 5995, 6035, 6040, 6060, 7170, 7200, 7325, 9650, 9670, 9715, 9760, 11760, 15205*
Middle East: *1260, 5965, 6040, 7200, 7205, 7325, 9660, 9740, 9760, 9770, 11760, 11920, 11925, 15185, 15205, 15260*
Africa: *621, 3990, 5995, 6035, 6040, 6045, 6080, 6095, 6125, 7170, 7195, 7280, 7325, 9530, 9540, 9550, 9575, 9620, 9670, 9745, 9760, 11720, 11835, 11840, 11915, 15205, 15240, 14410, 15415, 15445, 15580, 15600, 17715, 17785, 17870, 21485, 21660, 21680, 21840, 26000, 26040*
South America: *1580, 5995, 6130, 9455, 9650, 9690, 11580, 11675, 11740, 15205, 17640, 17730*
Australia and New Zealand: *6110, 11715, 11760, 15160, 15185, 15290, 15425, 17740*
South Asia: *1575, 6110, 7105, 7115, 7125, 7200, 7205, 9645, 9700, 9740, 9760, 11710, 11925, 15205, 15215, 15250, 15395, 17735, 17745, 21540*
East and South East Asia: *1575, 6110, 7230, 7275, 9565, 9760, 9770, 11715, 11760, 11775, 15160, 15185, 15290, 15425, 17740, 17820, 21460*

Deutsche Welle

North America: *5960, 6040, 6085, 6130, 6145, 9545, 9565, 9590, 11705, 11785*

SHORT WAVE RADIO FREQUENCIES

Radio Australia

North America: 9580, 15320, 15395, 17795
Europe: 6035, 7215, 9770, 11910, 15240

Radio Beijing

North America: 6160, 9820, 9860, 9880, 11650, 11860, 11945, 11970, 15120, 15385, 15520
Europe: 4130, 6860, 6995, 7590, 9860

Radio Japan

General: 9505, 9575, 9580, 9605, 9645, 9675, 11815, 11840, 11950, 15195, 15210, 15235, 15300, 17755, 17785, 17810, 17865, 21550, 21575, 21695
North America: 11710, 15195, 15300, 17825, 21610, 21640
Europe: 15235, 17785

Radio Canada International (English and French)

9555, 9625, 11720, 11915, 11925, 11935, 11945, 15150, 15315, 15325, 17820, 17875, 21695

Radio France International (English and French)

11705, 11730, 11845, 11930, 15155, 15200, 15300, 15313, 15360, 15425, 15435, 17720, 17845, 17850, 21515, 21525, 21580, 21675, 25900

Time Signals

4995-5005, 9995-10005, 14990-15010, 19990-20010, 24990-25010

TEMPERATURES WORLDWIDE

TEMPERATURES WORLDWIDE – average daily maximum in degrees C

Country	Town	Jan	Feb	Mar	Apr	May	Jun	Jul	Aug	Sep	Oct	Nov	Dec
Afghanistan	Kabul	2	4	12	19	26	31	33	33	29	23	17	8
Antigua	St John's	25	24	25	26	27	27	27	28	28	27	27	26
Argentina	Buenos Aires	29	28	26	22	18	14	14	16	18	21	24	28
Aruba	Oranjestad	28	29	29	30	30	31	31	31	32	31	30	29
Australia	Melbourne	26	26	24	20	17	14	13	15	17	19	22	24
Australia	Sydney	26	26	24	22	19	16	16	17	19	22	23	25
Austria	Vienna	1	3	8	14	19	22	24	23	19	13	7	3
Bahamas	Nassau	25	25	26	27	29	31	31	32	31	29	27	26
Bahrain	Al Manama	20	21	24	29	33	36	37	38	36	32	28	19
Barbados	Bridgetown	28	28	29	30	31	31	30	31	31	30	29	28
Belgium	Brussels	6	6	9	13	18	21	23	22	19	14	8	6
Bermuda	Hamilton	20	20	20	22	24	27	29	30	29	26	23	21
Bolivia	La Paz	16	16	17	17	17	16	17	17	17	18	19	18
Brazil	Rio de Janeiro	29	29	28	27	25	24	24	24	24	25	26	28
Bulgaria	Sofia	2	3	10	15	20	23	27	27	22	16	9	4
Burma	Rangoon	31	33	35	36	33	30	29	29	30	31	31	31
Canada	Montreal	-6	-5	1	10	18	23	26	24	19	12	4	-3
Canada	Toronto	8	8	13	23	28	32	33	33	31	24	17	10
Canada	Vancouver	5	7	10	14	18	21	23	23	18	14	9	6
Chile	Santiago	29	29	27	24	18	14	15	17	19	22	26	28
China	Beijing (Peking)	1	4	11	22	28	32	31	30	25	20	9	3
Colombia	Bogota	19	19	20	19	19	18	18	18	19	19	19	19

Country	Town	Jan	Feb	Mar	Apr	May	Jun	Jul	Aug	Sept	Oct	Nov	Dec
Cuba	Havana	26	26	27	29	30	32	31	30	31	29	27	26
Cyprus	Nicosia	14	16	18	24	29	34	37	37	33	28	22	17
Czechoslovakia	Prague	1	3	7	13	18	22	26	23	18	12	5	1
Denmark	Copenhagen	2	2	5	10	16	19	22	21	17	12	6	3
Dominican Republic	Santo Domingo	29	29	29	29	30	30	30	31	31	31	30	29
Egypt	Cairo	18	21	24	28	33	35	36	35	32	30	26	20
Falkland Islands	Port Stanley	13	13	12	9	7	5	4	5	7	9	11	12
Fiji	Suva	29	29	29	29	28	27	26	26	27	27	28	29
Finland	Helsinki	-6	-6	-4	3	9	14	17	16	11	5	1	-3
France	Paris	6	7	11	16	19	23	24	24	21	15	9	6
Gambia	Banjul	31	32	34	33	32	32	30	29	30	32	31	31
German Dem. Republic	Berlin	2	3	8	13	18	21	23	22	19	13	6	3
German Fed. Republic	Frankfurt	3	6	9	14	19	22	24	23	19	13	7	4
German Fed. Republic	Munich	1	3	9	14	18	20	23	22	20	13	7	2
Ghana	Accra	31	31	31	31	31	29	27	27	27	29	31	31
Gibraltar	Gibraltar	20	20	22	26	28	32	33	34	32	27	23	21
Greece	Athens	12	13	16	19	25	29	32	32	28	23	18	14
Hong Kong	Victoria	18	17	19	24	28	29	31	31	29	27	23	20
Hungary	Budapest	1	4	10	17	22	26	28	27	23	16	8	4
Iceland	Reykjavik	2	3	4	6	10	12	13	13	11	7	4	2
India	Bombay	28	28	30	32	33	32	29	29	29	32	32	31
India	Calcutta	27	29	34	36	36	33	32	32	32	32	29	26
India	Delhi	21	24	31	36	41	39	36	34	34	34	29	23

TEMPERATURES WORLDWIDE

Country	Town	Jan	Feb	Mar	Apr	May	Jun	Jul	Aug	Sept	Oct	Nov	Dec
Indonesia	Jakarta	29	29	30	31	31	31	31	31	31	31	30	29
Iran	Tehran	7	10	15	21	28	34	37	36	32	24	17	11
Iraq	Baghdad	16	18	22	29	36	41	43	43	40	33	25	18
Irish Republic	Dublin	8	8	10	13	15	18	20	19	17	14	10	8
Israel	Jerusalem	13	13	18	23	27	29	31	31	29	27	21	15
Italy	Rome	12	13	17	20	23	28	31	31	28	23	17	13
Italy	Venice	6	8	12	17	21	25	27	27	24	19	12	8
Jamaica	Kingston	32	32	32	32	33	33	34	34	34	33	33	32
Japan	Tokyo	8	9	12	17	21	24	28	30	26	21	16	11
Jordan	Amman	12	13	16	23	28	31	32	32	31	24	21	15
Kenya	Mombasa	30	30	32	32	29	28	28	28	29	30	31	29
Kenya	Nairobi	25	26	25	24	22	21	21	21	24	24	23	23
Korea	Seoul	0	3	8	17	22	27	29	31	26	19	11	3
Lebanon	Beirut	17	17	19	22	26	28	31	32	30	27	23	18
Libya	Tripoli	16	17	19	22	24	27	29	30	29	27	22	18
Macau	Macau	27	28	29	31	33	34	36	36	34	32	29	26
Malaysia	Kuala Lumpur	32	33	33	33	33	33	32	32	32	32	32	32
Malaysia	Penang	32	33	34	33	32	32	32	32	31	32	31	31
Mexico	Mexico City	19	21	24	25	26	24	23	23	23	21	20	19
Morocco	Rabat	17	18	20	22	23	26	28	28	27	25	21	18
Mozambique	Maputo	30	31	29	28	27	25	24	26	27	28	28	29
Nepal	Kathmandu	18	19	25	28	30	29	29	28	28	27	23	19
Netherlands	Amsterdam	4	5	8	11	16	18	21	20	18	13	5	5

TEMPERATURES WORLDWIDE

Country	Town	Jan	Feb	Mar	Apr	May	Jun	Jul	Aug	Sept	Oct	Nov	Dec
New Zealand	Auckland	23	23	22	19	17	14	13	14	16	17	18	21
New Zealand	Christchurch	21	21	19	17	13	11	10	11	14	17	19	21
Norway	Oslo	-1	0	4	10	17	21	23	21	16	9	3	-1
Oman	Muscat	25	25	28	32	37	38	36	33	34	34	30	20
Pakistan	Islamabad	16	19	24	31	37	40	36	34	24	32	28	20
Peru	Lima	28	28	28	27	23	20	19	19	20	22	23	26
Philippines	Manila	30	31	33	34	34	33	31	31	31	31	31	30
Poland	Warsaw	-1	0	5	12	19	22	24	23	18	12	4	0
Portugal	Lisbon	13	14	16	18	21	24	26	27	24	21	17	14
Qatar	Doha	26	29	32	37	40	40	42	42	40	36	33	28
Romania	Bucharest	1	4	10	18	23	27	30	30	25	18	10	4
Saudi Arabia	Riyadh	21	23	28	32	38	42	42	42	39	34	29	21
Seychelles	Port Victoria	28	29	29	30	29	28	27	27	28	28	29	28
Singapore	Singapore	30	31	31	31	32	31	31	31	31	31	31	31
South Africa	Johannesburg	26	25	24	22	19	17	17	20	23	25	25	26
Spain	Madrid	8	11	14	18	22	27	31	30	25	19	12	9
Sri Lanka	Colombo	30	31	31	31	31	29	29	29	29	29	29	29
Sweden	Stockholm	-1	-1	3	7	14	18	21	19	14	9	3	1
Switzerland	Zurich	3	6	10	14	20	23	25	24	21	14	7	3
Syria	Damascus	12	14	18	24	29	33	36	37	33	27	19	13
Taiwan	Taipei	19	18	21	25	28	32	33	33	31	27	24	21
Tanzania	Dar Es Salaam	27	27	27	27	28	28	28	29	29	29	27	26
Thailand	Bangkok	32	33	34	35	34	33	32	32	32	31	31	31

TEMPERATURES WORLDWIDE

Country	Town	Jan	Feb	Mar	Apr	May	Jun	Jul	Aug	Sept	Oct	Nov	Dec
Trinidad	Port of Spain	31	31	32	32	32	32	31	31	32	32	32	31
Tunisia	Tunis	14	16	18	21	24	29	32	33	31	25	20	16
Turkey	Istanbul	7	8	11	16	20	25	27	27	25	19	15	11
United Kingdom	London	7	7	11	13	17	21	23	22	19	14	9	7
Uraguay	Montevideo	28	28	26	22	18	15	14	15	17	20	23	26
USA	Miami	23	24	26	27	29	30	31	31	31	28	26	24
USA	New York	3	3	7	14	20	25	28	27	26	21	11	5
USA	San Francisco	13	15	16	17	17	19	18	18	21	20	17	14
USSR	Moscow	-6	-5	0	8	18	23	24	22	16	8	-1	-5
Venezuela	Caracas	24	25	26	27	27	26	26	26	27	26	25	26
Viet Nam	Hanoi	20	21	23	28	32	33	32	32	31	29	26	22
Yugoslavia	Belgrade	3	5	11	18	23	26	28	28	24	18	11	5
Zaire	Kinshasa	31	31	32	32	31	29	27	28	31	31	31	30
Zambia	Lusaka	26	26	26	26	25	23	23	25	29	31	29	27
Zimbabwe	Harare	26	26	26	26	23	21	21	23	26	27	27	26

TIME ZONES

TIME ZONES – *Countries A to Z in relation to Greenwich Mean Time, showing summer daylight saving times where appropriate.*

Afghanistan	4½ hours ahead
Albania	2 hours ahead
Algeria	1 hour ahead
Andorra	2 hours ahead
Angola	1 hour ahead
Anguilla	4 hours behind
Antigua/Barbuda	4 hours behind
Argentina	3 hours behind
Aruba	4 hours behind
Australia –	
Western Australia	8 hours ahead
Northern Territory, South	
Australia, Broken Hill, NSW	9½ hours ahead
Australian Capital Territory,	
New South Wales (except	
Broken Hill), Queensland,	
Tasmania, Victoria	10 hours ahead
Lord Howe Island	10½ hours ahead
Austria	2 hours ahead
Azores	GMT
Bahamas	4 hours behind
Bahrain	3 hours ahead
Bangladesh	6 hours ahead
Barbados	4 hours behind
Belgium	2 hours ahead
Belize	6 hours behind
Benin	1 hour ahead
Bermuda	3 hours behind
Bhutan	5½ hours ahead
Bolivia	4 hours behind
Botswana	2 hours ahead
Brazil –	
Fernando de Noronha	2 hours behind
Brasilia, East and coast	3 hours behind
West	4 hours behind
State of Acre	5 hours behind
Brunei Darussalam	8 hours ahead
Bulgaria	3 hours ahead
Burkina Faso	GMT
Burma	6½ hours ahead
Burundi	2 hours ahead
Cameroon Republic	1 hour ahead
Canada –	
Newfoundland	2½ hours behind
Atlantic Time	3 hours behind
Eastern Time	4 hours behind
Central Time	5 hours behind
Mountain Time	6 hours behind
Pacific Time, Yukon	7 hours behind
Canary Islands	2 hours ahead
Cape Verde Islands	1 hour behind
Cayman Islands	5 hours behind
Central African Republic	1 hour ahead
Chad	1 hour ahead
Chile	4 hours behind
China	9 hours ahead

Colombia	5 hours behind
Comoros	3 hours ahead
Congo People's Republic	1 hour ahead
Cook Islands	10 hours behind
Costa Rica	6 hours behind
Cuba	4 hours behind
Cyprus	3 hours ahead
Czechoslovakia	2 hours ahead
Denmark	2 hours ahead
Djibouti	3 hours ahead
Dominica	4 hours behind
Dominican Republic	4 hours behind
Easter Island	6 hours behind
Ecuador	5 hours behind
Egypt	2 hours ahead
El Salvador	6 hours behind
Equatorial Guinea	1 hour ahead
Ethiopia	3 hours ahead
Falkland Islands	4 hours behind
Faroe Islands	1 hour ahead
Fiji	12 hours ahead
Finland	3 hours ahead
France	2 hours ahead
French West Indies	4 hours behind
Gabon	1 hour ahead
Galapagos Islands	6 hours behind
Gambia	GMT
East Germany	2 hours ahead
West Germany	2 hours ahead
Ghana	GMT
Gibraltar	2 hours ahead
Greece	3 hours ahead
Greenland	3 hours behind
Grenada	4 hours behind
Guadeloupe	4 hours behind
Guam	10 hours ahead
Guatemala	6 hours behind
Guiana, French	3 hours behind
Guinea Republic	GMT
Guinea Bissau	GMT
Guyana	3 hours behind
Haiti	4 hours behind
Honduras	6 hours behind
Hong Kong	8 hours ahead
Hungary	2 hours ahead
Iceland	GMT
India	5½ hours ahead
Indonesia —	
West Zone — Java, Sumatra, Bali	7 hours ahead
Central Zone — Kalimantan, Sulawesi, Nusa Tenggara	8 hours ahead
East Zone — Maluku, Irian Jaya	9 hours ahead
Iran	3½ hours ahead
Iraq	4 hours ahead
Irish Republic	1 hour ahead
Israel	3 hours ahead
Italy	2 hours ahead
Ivory Coast	GMT

Jamaica	5 hours behind
Japan	9 hours ahead
Jordan	3 hours ahead
Kampuchea	7 hours ahead
Kenya	3 hours ahead
Kiribati Republic	12 hours ahead
Korea Democratic People's Rep.	9 hours ahead
Korea Republic	10 hours ahead
Kuwait	3 hours ahead
Laos (Lao)	7 hours ahead
Lebanon	3 hours ahead
Lesotho	2 hours ahead
Liberia	GMT
Libya	2 hours ahead
Luxembourg	2 hours ahead
Macao	8 hours ahead
Madagascar	3 hours ahead
Madeira	GMT
Malawi	2 hours ahead
Malaysia	8 hours ahead
Maldive Islands	5 hours ahead
Mali	GMT
Malta	2 hours ahead
Mauritania	GMT
Mauritius	4 hours ahead
Mexico —	
General Mexico Time	6 hours behind
Lower California,	
North Pacific Coast,	
Baja California Norte	7 hours behind
Monaco	2 hours ahead
Mongolia	9 hours ahead
Montserrat	4 hours behind
Morocco	GMT
Mozambique	2 hours ahead
Namibia	2 hours ahead
Nauru	12 hours ahead
Nepal	5½ hours ahead
Netherlands	2 hours ahead
Netherlands Antilles	4 hours behind
New Caledonia	11 hours ahead
New Zealand	12 hours ahead
Nicaragua	6 hours behind
Niger	1 hour ahead
Nigeria	1 hour ahead
Niue	11 hours behind
Norfolk Island	11½ hours ahead
Norway	2 hours ahead
Oman	4 hours ahead
Pakistan	5 hours ahead
Palau	9 hours ahead
Panama	5 hours behind
Papua New Guinea	10 hours ahead
Paraguay	4 hours behind
Peru	5 hours behind
Philippines	8 hours ahead
Pitcairn Island	8½ hours behind
Poland	2 hours ahead
Polynesia, French	10 hours behind
Portugal	1 hour ahead

Puerto Rico	4 hours behind
Qatar	3 hours ahead
Reunion Islands	4 hours ahead
Romania	3 hours ahead
Rwanda	2 hours ahead
Saint Helena	GMT
Saint Kitts and Nevis	4 hours behind
Saint Lucia	4 hours behind
Saint Vincent and Grenadines	4 hours behind
Samoa	11 hours behind
Sao Tome and Principe	GMT
Saudi Arabia	3 hours ahead
Senegal	GMT
Seychelles	4 hours ahead
Sierra Leone	GMT
Singapore	8 hours ahead
Solomon Islands	11 hours ahead
Somalia	3 hours ahead
South Africa	2 hours ahead
Spain	2 hours ahead
Sri Lanka	5½ hours ahead
Sudan	2 hours ahead
Suriname	3 hours behind
Swaziland	2 hours ahead
Sweden	2 hours ahead
Switzerland	2 hours ahead
Syria	3 hours ahead
Taiwan	8 hours ahead
Tanzania	3 hours ahead
Thailand	7 hours ahead
Togo	GMT
Tonga	13 hours ahead
Trinidad and Tobago	4 hours behind
Tunisia	1 hour ahead
Turkey	3 hours ahead
Turks and Caicos Islands	4 hours behind
Tuvalu Republic	12 hours ahead
Uganda	3 hours ahead
United Arab Emirates	4 hours ahead
USA —	
Eastern Time	4 hours behind
Central Time, Indiana	5 hours behind
Mountain Time	6 hours behind
Pacific Time, Arizona	7 hours behind
Alaska (except Aleutian Is. west of 169.3 degrees West)	8 hours behind
Aleutian Is. (west of 169.3 degrees West)	9 hours behind
Hawaiian Islands	10 hours behind
USSR —	
Tallin, Riga, Vilnius, Kiev, Leningrad, Moscow	4 hours ahead
Arkhangelsk, Volgograd, Tbilisi	5 hours ahead
Ashkhabad, Sverdlovsk	6 hours ahead
Alma-Ata, Omsk, Salekhard	7 hours ahead
Novosibirsk, Krasnoyarsk	8 hours ahead
Irkutsk	9 hours ahead
Yakutsk	10 hours ahead
Khabarovsk, Vladivostok	11 hours ahead

TIME ZONES

Magadan, Sakhalin Island	12 hours ahead
Petropavlovsk, Kamchatskiy	13 hours ahead
Anadyr	14 hours ahead
Uruguay	3 hours behind
Vanuatu Republic	11 hours ahead
Venezuela	4 hours behind
Viet Nam	7 hours ahead
Virgin Islands	4 hours behind
Yemen Democratic Rep. (South)	3 hours ahead
Yemen Arab Rep. (North)	3 hours ahead
Yugoslavia	2 hours ahead
Zaire —	
Bandundu, Bas-Zaire, Kinshasa, Mbandaka	1 hour ahead
Haut-Zaire, Kasai, Kivu, Shaba	2 hours ahead
Zambia	2 hours ahead
Zimbabwe	2 hours ahead

USEFUL ADDRESSES

F − Footwear
R − Rucksacks
B − Sleeping Bags
S − Stoves
T − Tents
W − Waterproofs, Travel Clothes and Warmwear

W	Belstaff International Ltd., Caroline Street, Longton, Stoke on Trent, ST3 1DD
F R W	Berghaus, 34 Dean Street, Newcastle upon Tyne, NE1 1PG
W B	Buffalo Sleeping Bags, Unit 20, Meersbrook Works, Valley Road, Sheffield, S8 9FT
W	Bradsport Ltd., Camroyd Street, Dewsbury, WF13 1PG
B	Brett Harris Ltd., Waterloo Mills, Silsden, BD20 0HA
W	Calange, Harditex House, Davenport Avenue, Withington, Manchester, M20 9EZ
S	Camping Gaz International, 126130 St. Leonards Road, Windsor, SL4 3DG
T	Clyde Canvas Goods Structures Ltd., 166 Handford Road, Ipswich
R	Cobles, 74 Backchurch Lane, London, E1 1LX
S	Coleman UK Inc., Parish Wharf Estate, Harbour Road, Portishead, Bristol
T	Conquest Tents, Unit 13, Quay Lane, Gosport, PO12 4LT
W	Craghoppers, Bradford Road, Birstall, Batley, WF17 4DH
F	Croft Footwear Ltd., Croft Mill, Belfield Road, Rochdale, OL16 2UT
R W	Cumbrian Leisure Ltd., Kingstown Broadway, Carlisle, CA3 0HA
F	Daisy Roots, Westfield Trading Estate, Midsomer Norton, Bath, Avon
S	Epigas International Ltd., Viaduct Mill, Chestergate, Stockport, SK3 0AJ
F R W	Europa Mountain Sport, Ann Street, Kendal, LA9 6AB
R WTB	Fjällräven UK Ltd., Priestly Way, Staples Corner, London, NW2 7AZ
F	G.T. Hawkins Ltd., Overstone Road, Northampton, NN1 3JJ
F	Giffard Newton & Sons Ltd., Townsend Road, Chesham, HP5 2AD
T	John James Hawley Ltd., Lichfield Road, Walsall, WS4 2HX
W	Helly-Hansen (UK) Ltd., College Street, Kempston, Bedford, MK42 8NA
W	Henri-Lloyd Ltd., Smithfold Lane, Worsley, Manchester, M28 6AR
F	Hi-Tec Sports Ltd., 2426 Towerfield Road, Shoeburyness, Essex
R W B	Karrimor International Ltd., Avenue Parade, Accrington, BB5 6PR
W	Mileta Sports Ltd., Spen Vale Mills, Station Lane, Heckmondwike, West Yorks.

USEFUL ADDRESSES

F R WTB	Mountaineering Activities Ltd., MOAC House, Demmings Road Industrial Estate, Cheadle, SK8 2PE
F WTB	Mountain Equipment Ltd., Leech Street, Stalybridge, SK15 1SD
W	North Cape (Scotland) Ltd., Cunningham Road, Springkerse Industrial Estate, Stirling, FK7 7SW
R WTB	Northern Feather Leisure (UK) Ltd., Unit 14 Greenholme Mills, Iron Row, Burley in Wharfedale, LS29 7DB
R S	AB Optimus Ltd., Sanders Lodge Estate, Rushden, NN10 9BQ
W	Peter Storm Ltd., 14 High Pavement, Nottingham, NG1 1HP
WTB	Phoenix Mountaineering Ltd., Coquetdale Trading Estate, Amble, Morpeth, Northumberland, NE65 0PG
S	Primus-Sievert UK Ltd., PO Box No.562, 911 Gleneldon Road, Streatham, SW16 2AU
W	Rohan Designs plc, 30 Maryland Road, Tongwell, Milton Keynes, MK15 8HN
R W B	Sanctuary Mountain Sports Ltd., 20 Greys Court, Kingsland Grange, Woolston, Warrington, WA1 4SH
T B	Robert Saunders (Chigwell) Ltd., Five Oaks Lane, Chigwell, Essex, IG7 4QP
W T	Snowdon Clothing, Goodman Street, Llanberis, Gwynedd, LL55 4HN
B	Snuggledown of Norway (UK) Ltd., 39 Burners Lane, Kiln Farm, Milton Keynes, MK11 3HJ
W	Sprayway Ltd., 16 Chester Street, Manchester, M1 5GE
F R WTB	Survival Aids Ltd., Morland, nr. Penrith, Cumbria, CA10 3AZ
B	T36.9, Cambuslang Road, Farme Cross, Rutherglen, Glasgow, G73 1RS
F	Thomas H. Loveday Ltd., Islip, Kettering, NN14 3LW
F R WTB	The North Face (Scotland) Ltd., PO Box 16, Industrial Estate, Port Glasgow, PA14 5XL
F	Timberland, 133 Westbourne Grove, London, W11 2RS
W	Travelling Light, Morland House, Morland, Penrith, CA10 1BR
R W	Troll Safety Equipment Ltd., Spring Mill, Uppermill, nr. Oldham, OL3 6AA
R WTB	Ultimate Equipment Ltd., Walnut Street, Halifax, HX1 4DL
F R WTB	Vango (Scotland) Ltd., 70 East Hamilton Street, Ladyburn, Greenock, PA15 2UB
R WTB	VauDe (UK) Ltd., PO Box 10, Hexham, NE46 1TE
W	Walrus Waterproofs, Mersey Street, Bulwell, Nottingham, NG6 8JA
W	Walsden Weatherwear Ltd., 29 Embleton Crescent, North Shields, Tyne and Wear, NE29 8BW
W	Warm 'n Dry, 138 Lancaster Road, Enfield, Middlesex
W	Westcroft, Unit 1 Knighton Heath Estate, Ringwood Road, West Howe, Bournemouth, BH11 8NE
R WTB	Wild Country, Townhead, Eyam, Derbyshire, S30 1RD
W	Yoredale Weather Wear Ltd., 3 Well Lane, Batley, WF17 5HQ

USEFUL ADDRESSES

Mail Order:

Rohan, 30 Maryland Road, Tongwell, Milton Keynes, MK15
8HN. Telephone: 0908 618888

Field and Trek (Equipment) Ltd., 3 Wates Way, Brentwood,
Essex, CM15 9TB. Telephone: 0277 221259

Freewheel, PO Box 740, London, NW2 7JQ. Telephone: 01 450
0768

Survival Aids Ltd., Morland, Penrith, Cumbria, CA10 3AZ.
Telephone: 09314 444

Travelling Light, Morland House, Morland, Penrith, Cumbria,
CA10 3AZ. Telephone: 09314 488

Organisations

Youth Hostels Association, Trevelyan House, 8 St. Stephen's
Hill, St. Albans, Hertfordshire, AL1 2DY. Telephone: 0727
55215

Camping and Caravanning Club, 11 Grosvenor Place, London,
SW1 0EY. Telephone: 01 828 1012

Cyclists Touring Club, 69 Meadrow, Godalming, Surrey, GU7
3HS. Telephone: 04868 7217

British Mountaineering Council, Crawford House, Precinct
Centre, Booth Street East, Manchester, M13 9RZ.
Telephone: 061 273 5835

The Vegetarian Society of the United Kingdom Ltd., Parkdale,
Dunham Road, Altrincham, WA14 4QG. Telephone: 061
928 0793

Miscellaneous

Immunisation Centres

British Airways

75 Regent Street, London, SW1. Telephone: 01 439 9584

Speedbird House, Heathrow Airport. Telephone: 01 562
5433

101/102 Cheapside, London, EC2. Telephone: 01 606 2977

Thomas Cook Vaccination Centre, 45 Berkeley Street, London,
W1A 1EB. Telephone: 01 499 4000

Trailfinders, 48 Earls Court Road, London, W8 6EJ. Telephone:
01 937 9631

West London Vaccination Centre, 53 Great Cumberland Place,
London, W1. Telephone: 01 262 6456

Maps

Stanfords International Map Centre, 12-14 Long Acre, London,
WC2P 9LP. Telephone: 01 836 1321

McCarta Ltd., The Map and Guide Shop, 122 King's Cross Road,
London, WC1X 9DS. Telephone: 01 278 8278

The Geo Centre, Internationales Landkartenhaus, 7 Stuttgart
80, (Vaihingen), Honigiveisenstrasse 25, Postfach 80 08 30,
D-7000 Stuttgart, West Germany.

Malaria Reference Laboratory, London School of Hygiene and
Tropical Medicine, Keppel Street, London, WC1E 7HT.
Telephone: 01 636 7921

MASTA Ltd. (Medical Advisory Service for Travellers Abroad),
Keppel Street, London, WC1E 7HT. Telephone: 01 631 4408

Europ Assistance, 252 High Street, Croydon, CR0 1QH.
Telephone: 01 680 1234

VACCINATION REQUIREMENTS – *Countries A to Z*

Key:
   r – *Vaccinations or tablets recommended.*
   E – *Vaccinations essential. You will be required to produce a certificate.*

Yellow Fever column
   r – *Vaccination recommended. Infants under nine months should not be vaccinated, or exposed to the disease.*
E1 – *Vaccination essential. Infants under one year exempt, but note r above.*
E2 – *Vaccination essential. Infants under one year exempt, but note r above. Travellers arriving from non-infected areas and staying less than two weeks exempt.*
   ∗ – *Vaccination essential if traveller arrives from an infected country.*

Country	Malaria	Cholera	Typhoid	Polio	Yellow Fever
Afghanistan	r	r	r	r	∗
Albania					∗
Algeria	r		r	r	∗
Angola	r	r	r	r	E1
Antigua/Barbuda			r	r	∗
Argentina	r		r	r	
Australia					∗
Austria					
Azores					
Bahamas			r	r	∗
Bahrain		r	r	r	∗
Bangladesh	r	r	r	r	∗
Barbados			r	r	∗
Belgium					
Belize	r		r	r	∗
Benin	r	r	r	r	E1
Bermuda					
Bhutan	r	r	r	r	∗
Bolivia	r		r	r	r
Botswana	r	r	r	r	
Brazil	r		r	r	∗r
Brunei		r	r	r	∗
Bulgaria					
Burkino Faso	r	r	r	r	E1
Burma	r	r	r	r	∗
Burundi	r	r	r	r	∗
Cameroon	r	r	r	r	E1
Canada					
Canary Islands					
Cape Verde Islands	r		r	r	∗
Cayman Islands			r	r	
Central African Republic	r	r	r	r	E1
Chad	r	r	r	r	E1
Chile			r	r	
China	r		r	r	∗
Colombia	r		r	r	r

VACCINATION REQUIREMENTS

Country	Malaria	Cholera	Typhoid	Polio	Yellow Fever
Comoros	r		r	r	
Congo	r	r	r	r	E2
Cook Islands			r	r	
Costa Rica	r		r	r	
Cuba			r	r	
Cyprus					
Czechoslovakia					
Denmark					
Djibouti	r	r	r	r	*
Dominica			r	r	*
Dominican Republic	r		r	r	
Ecuador	r		r	r	
Egypt	r	r	r	r	*
El Salvador	r		r	r	*
Equatorial Guinea	r	r	r	r	*r
Ethiopia	r	r	r	r	*r
Falkland Islands			r	r	
Fiji			r	r	*
Finland					
France					
Gabon	r	r	r	r	*r
Gambia	r	r	r	r	E1
Germany, East					
Germany, West					
Ghana	r	r	r	r	*r
Gibraltar					
Greece					*
Greenland					
Grenada			r	r	*
Guam			r	r	*
Guatemala	r		r	r	*
Guiana, French	r		r	r	E2r
Guinea	r	r	r	r	*r
Guinea Bissau	r	r	r	r	*r
Guyana	r		r	r	*r
Haiti	r		r	r	*
Honduras	r		r	r	*
Hong Kong			r	r	
Hungary					
Iceland					
India	r	r	r	r	*
Indonesia/Bali	r	r	r	r	*
Iran	r		r	r	*
Iraq	r	r	r	r	*
Irish Republic					
Israel			r	r	
Italy					
Ivory Coast	r	r	r	r	E1
Jamaica			r	r	*
Japan			r	r	
Jordan		r	r	r	
Kampuchea	r	r	r	r	*
Kenya	r	r	r	r	*r
Kiribati			r	r	*
Korea (North)		r	r	r	
Korea (South)		r	r	r	
Kuwait		r	r	r	
Laos (Lao)	r	r	r	r	*

VACCINATION REQUIREMENTS

Country	Malaria	Cholera	Typhoid	Polio	Yellow Fever
Lebanon		r	r	r	*
Lesotho		r	r	r	*
Liberia	r	r	r	r	*r
Libya	r	r	r	r	*
Luxembourg					
Madagascar	r	r	r	r	*
Madeira					
Malawi	r	r	r	r	*
Malaysia	r	r	r	r	*
Maldives	r	r	r	r	*
Mali	r	r	r	r	E2r
Malta					*
Mauritania	r	r	r	r	E2r
Mauritius	r		r		*
Mexico	r		r	r	*
Monaco					
Mongolia			r	r	
Montserrat			r	r	*
Morocco	r	r	r	r	
Mozambique	r	r	r	r	*
Namibia	r	r	r	r	*r
Nauru			r	r	*
Nepal	r	r	r	r	*
Netherlands					
Netherlands Antilles			r	r	*
New Caledonia			r	r	*
New Zealand					
Nicaragua	r		r	r	
Niger	r	E	r	r	E1
Nigeria	r	r	r	r	E1
Niue			r	r	*
Norway					
Oman	r	r	r	r	*
Pakistan	r	r	r	r	*
Panama	r		r	r	E1
Papua New Guinea	r	r	r	r	*
Paraguay	r		r	r	*
Peru	r		r	r	*r
Philippines	r	r	r	r	*
Pitcairn Island			r	r	*
Poland					
Polynesia, French			r	r	*
Portugal					
Puerto Rico			r	r	
Qatar		E	r	r	*
Reunion Islands			r		*
Romania					
Rwanda	r	r	r	r	E1
Saint Helena			r	r	
Saint Lucia			r	r	*
Saint Vincent/Grenadines			r	r	*
Samoa			r	r	*
Sao Tome and Principe	r	r	r	r	E2
Saudi Arabia	r	r	r	r	*
Senegal	r	r	r	r	E1
Seychelles			r	r	
Sierra Leone	r	r	r	r	E1
Singapore		r	r	r	*
Solomon Islands	r		r	r	*

VACCINATION REQUIREMENTS

Country	*Malaria*	*Cholera*	*Typhoid*	*Polio*	*Yellow Fever*
Somalia	r	r	r	r	✻r
South Africa	r	r	r	r	✻
Spain					
Sri Lanka	r	r	r	r	✻
Sudan	r	r	r	r	✻r
Surinam	r		r	r	✻
Swaziland	r	r	r	r	✻
Sweden					
Switzerland					
Syria	r	r	r	r	✻
Taiwan		r	r	r	
Tanzania	r	r	r	r	✻r
Thailand	r	r	r	r	✻
Togo	r	r	r	r	E1
Trinidad and Tobago			r	r	✻
Tunisia		r	r	r	✻
Turkey	r	r	r	r	
Tuvalu			r	r	✻
Uganda	r	r	r	r	E1
United Arab Emirates	r	r	r	r	✻
USA					
USSR					
Uruguay			r	r	
Vanuatu	r		r	r	
Venezuela	r		r	r	r
Vietnam	r	r	r	r	✻
Virgin Islands			r	r	
West Indies Ass. States			r	r	
French West Indies			r	r	
Yemen Dem. Rep.	r	r	r	r	✻
Yemen Arab Republic	r	r	r	r	✻
Yugoslavia					
Zaire	r	r	r	r	✻r
Zambia	r	r	r	r	✻r
Zimbabwe	r	r	r	r	✻

VISA REQUIREMENTS FOR BRITISH NATIONALS – Countries A to Z

Note that the requirements listed are for holders of passports stamped 'British Subject: Citizen of the United Kingdom and Colonies'. They do not necessarily apply to holders of British Passports issued overseas.

COUNTRY	VISA?	REMARKS
Afghanistan	Yes	Allow 48 hours for issue.
Albania	Yes	Business and group visas only, minimum 20 people.
Algeria	No	If stay more than 3 months, permit de séjour required.
Andorra	No	
Angola	Yes	Allow 2 weeks for issue.
Anguilla	No	
Antigua/Barbuda	No	Return ticket essential.
Argentina	Yes	Allow 7 days for issue.
Australia	Yes	
Austria	No	No visa for stays up to 6 months.
Azores	No	
Bahamas	No	
Bahrain	No	
Bangladesh	Yes	Allow 36 hours for issue.
Barbados	No	
Belgium	No	
Belize	No	
Benin	Yes	Valid 7 days.
Bermuda	No	Return ticket essential.

COUNTRY	VISA?	REMARKS
Bhutan	Yes	Allow 10 weeks minimum for issue.
Bolivia	No	Tourists don't need visas, other visitors do.
Botswana	No	
Brazil	No	Return ticket essential, plus funds to meet expenses.
Brunei Darussalam	No	
Bulgaria	Yes	If travelling independently. Allow 10 days for issue.
Burkino Faso	Yes	Allow 24 hours for issue. Return ticket also required.
Burma	Yes	Tourist visas valid for 7 days only. Allow 48 hours for issue.
Burundi	Yes	Allow 48 hours for issue. Return or onward ticket also required.
Cameroon Republic	Yes	Allow 48 hours for issue.
Canada	No	
Cape Verde Islands	Yes	Allow 2 to 3 weeks for issue. Return or onward ticket required.
Cayman Islands	No	Return or onward ticket required.
Central African Republic	Yes	Application should be made to French Consulate. Allow 48 hours for issue.
Chad	Yes	Application should be made to French Consulate. Allow 24 hours for issue.
Chile	No	
China	Yes	Allow 3 days for issue.
Colombia	No	Valid passport and return or continuation ticket essential.
Comoros	Yes	Issued on arrival.
Congo People's Republic	Yes	Allow 3 weeks for issue. Tourists must show evidence of hotel reservations.
Cook Islands	No	Valid passport and return ticket essential. Visa required after 31 days.
Costa Rica	No	
Cuba	Yes	Personal letter of application required. Allow 3 weeks for issue.
Cyprus	No	

COUNTRY	VISA?	REMARKS
Czechoslovakia	Yes	Allow 24 to 48 hours for issue.
Denmark	No	Visa required for stays over 3 months.
Djibouti	Yes	Allow 48 hours for issue.
Dominica	Yes	Issued on arrival. Return or onward ticket required.
Dominican Republic	No	Except British passport holders of Chinese descent and those born in Hong Kong.
Ecuador	No	Visa required for stays over 3 months.
Egypt	Yes	Issued on arrival.
El Salvador	No	
Equatorial Guinea	Yes	Apply to Embassy in Paris. Allow 2 months minimum for issue.
Ethiopia	Yes	Allow 4 weeks for issue. Return or onward ticket required.
Falkland Islands	No	
Faroe Islands	No	Visa required for stays over 3 months.
Fiji	No	Return or onward ticket required.
Finland	No	
France	No	Visa required for stays over 3 months.
Gabon	Yes	Allow 15 days for issue. Company letter required for business visa.
Gambia	No	Visa required for stays over 3 months.
German Democratic Republic (East)	Yes	Transit visas can be purchased at border crossings.
German Federal Republic (West)	No	Visa required for stays over 3 months.
Ghana	Yes	Entry permit required, company letter and return ticket.
Gibraltar	No	
Greece	No	Visa required for stays over 3 months.
Greenland	No	Maximum stay 3 months. Return ticket and sufficient funds for stay essential.
Grenada	No	

COUNTRY	VISA?	REMARKS
Guatemala	Yes	Apply El Salvador Embassy. Allow 48 hours for issue.
Guiana, French	No	Return ticket required.
Guinea Republic	Yes	Tourist visas granted occasionally. Apply to Embassy in Paris. Allow 4 to 5 weeks.
Guinea Bissau	Yes	Allow 48 hours for issue.
Guyana	Yes	Allow 7 days for issue.
Haiti	No	Tourist card must be obtained on arrival.
Honduras Republic	No	Visa only required if on business.
Hong Kong	No	Visa required for stays over 6 months.
Hungary	Yes	Allow 24 hours for issue. Passport must be valid for minimum of 6 months.
Iceland	No	Return ticket essential.
India	Yes	Allow 24 hours for issue.
Indonesia/Bali	No	Return ticket essential. Visit without visa for tourist purposes only.
Iran	Yes	Allow 7 days for issue.
Iraq	Yes	Allow 3 days for issue.
Irish Republic	No	
Israel	No	
Italy	No	
Ivory Coast	No	
Jamaica	No	Visa required for stays over 3 months.
Japan	No	Visa required for stays over 3 months.
Jordan	Yes	Allow 48 hours for issue.
Kenya	No	
Kiribati Republic	No	Up to 21 days.
Korea (Democratic Peoples Rep.)	Yes	Allow 1 month for issue.

COUNTRY	VISA?	REMARKS
Korea	No	Up to 60 days.
Kuwait	Yes	Valid 28 days. Allow 24 hours for issue.
Laos (Lao)	Yes	Permission required from Ministry of Foreign Affairs, Vientiane. Allow 4 to 6 weeks.
Lebanon	Yes	Business letter required stating nature of business. Allow 48 hours for issue.
Lesotho	No	
Liberia	Yes	Business letter required stating nature of business. Allow 24 hours for issue.
Libya	Yes	Visitors must be in possession of US$500 or equivalent.
Luxembourg	No	Visa required for stays over 3 months.
Macao	No	
Madagascar	Yes	Return ticket or evidence of sufficient funds required.
Malawi	No	Up to 6 months. Return ticket required.
Maldives	Yes	Valid 30 days.
Mali	Yes	Valid 1 month. Allow 48 hours for issue.
Malta	No	
Mauritania	Yes	Allow 24 hours for issue.
Mauritius	No	
Mexico	No	Tourist card required, available free of charge.
Mongolia	Yes	Allow 2 weeks for issue. Application through travel agent arranging travel.
Morocco	No	
Mozambique	Yes	Allow 1 to 2 weeks for issue. Company letter required stating reasons for visit.
Nauru	Yes	Return or onward ticket required.
Nepal	Yes	Valid 3 months. Allow 24 hours for issue.
Netherlands	No	Visa required for stays over 3 months.
Netherlands Antilles	No	

COUNTRY	VISA?	REMARKS
New Caledonia	No	Return or onward ticket required.
New Zealand	No	Visa required for stays over 6 months. Onward ticket and sufficient funds required.
Nicaragua	No	Maximum stay 3 months. Onward or return ticket required.
Niger	No	Onward or return ticket required.
Nigeria	Yes	Allow 3 days for issue. Entry permit required.
Niue	No	Up to 30 days. Proof of sufficient funds and return or onward ticket required.
Norway	No	
Oman	No	7 day business visa only. Visitors need a sponsor in Oman.
Pakistan	Yes	Allow 4 days for issue.
Panama Republic	No	
Papua New Guinea	No	Up to 30 days. Return ticket essential.
Paraguay	No	Tourist card issued on arrival.
Peru	No	
Philippines	No	Up to 21 days provided you have onward ticket. Longer stays require visa.
Poland	Yes	Allow 10 days for issue.
Polynesia, French	No	Return ticket required.
Portugal	No	Visa required for stays over 2 months.
Qatar	No	
Reunion Islands	No	
Romania	Yes	Allow 48 hours for issue.
Rwanda	Yes	Allow 72 hours for issue. Certificate of moral conduct required.
Saint Kitts and Nevis	No	
Saint Lucia	No	
Saint Vincent and Grenadines	No	

VISA REQUIREMENTS

COUNTRY	VISA?	REMARKS
Samoa	No	Entry permit required from New Zealand Govt. of Maori & Island Affairs.
Sao Tome and Principe	Yes	
Saudi Arabia	Yes	No tourist visas.
Senegal	Yes	Allow 48 hours for issue. Return ticket also required.
Seychelles	No	Visitor's permit issued on arrival.
Sierra Leone	Yes	Allow 72 hours for issue.
Singapore	No	Evidence of sufficient funds, return or onward ticket required.
Solomon Islands	No	
Somalia	Yes	Allow 2 to 3 days for issue.
South Africa	No	Return ticket required.
Spain	No	Visa required for stays over 90 days.
Sri Lanka	No	Up to 6 months.
Sudan	Yes	Tourist visa applications must include return air tickets and travellers cheques.
Suriname	No	
Swaziland	No	
Sweden	No	
Switzerland	No	
Syria	Yes	Visas not being granted to British passport holders at time of going to press.
Taiwan	Yes	Allow 24 hours for issue.
Tanzania	No	Visitors pass must be obtained prior to entry.
Thailand	Yes	Allow 24 hours for issue.
Togo	Yes	Allow 48 hours for issue.
Tonga	No	
Trinidad and Tobago	No	

COUNTRY	VISA?	REMARKS
Tunisia	No	Visa required for stays over 3 months.
Turkey	No	
Tuvalu Republic	No	Allow 5 days for issue.
Uganda	Yes	
United Arab Emirates	No	Issued same day if applied for in person. Otherwise allow 10 days.
USA	Yes	Allow 2 weeks for issue.
USSR	Yes	
Uruguay	No	
Vanuatu Republic	No	Tourists must possess Tourist Card issued by carrier, plus return or onward ticket.
Venezuela	No	Visitors must have sponsor in Viet Nam. Allow 4 to 6 weeks for issue of visa.
Viet Nam	Yes	
Virgin Islands, British	No	Also evidence to prove you will be leaving the country.
Virgin Islands, US	Yes	Return ticket required.
French West Indies	No	Allow 48 hours for issue.
Yemen Democratic Republic (South)	Yes	Allow 48 hours for issue.
Yemen Arab Republic	Yes	Up to 3 months.
Yugoslavia	No	Allow 48 hours for issue.
Zaire	Yes	Return ticket required.
Zambia	No	Return ticket required.
Zimbabwe	No	

INDEX

DO-IT-YOURSELF DOCUMENT LIST

Just to show you what a nice chap I am, I've saved you the trouble of writing out all the boring bits of a list of your important documents etc., which you ought to note down. It will help if you fill it in, though. And for frequent travellers, this is the one page of the book which you CAN photocopy!

Name: ....

Address: ....

....

....

Telephone: ....

Passport Number: ....

Driving Licence: ....

Traveller's Cheques

   Numbers: ....

....

   Emergency refunds from: ....

....

Travel Ticket Numbers: ....

....

Travel Insurance

   Certificate Number: ....

   24 hour emergency telephone: ....

Credit card

   Numbers: ....

....

   24 hour telephone: ....

Next of kin

   Name: ....

   Address: ....

....

....

....

   Telephone: ....

Next of kin

   Name: ....

   Address: ....

....

....

....

   Telephone: ....

ABOUT THE AUTHOR — *if you're sure you want to know!*

Clive Tully is a freelance journalist, photographer and broadcaster, specialising in outdoors leisure and travel. As Equipment Editor of 'The Great Outdoors', his entertaining but frank reviews of clothing and equipment for walking and camping have in many cases been instrumental in improving the general standard of outdoors equipment. His travel articles have appeared in national newspapers and general interest magazines. He can also be heard on 'Sound Advice' audio travel cassettes.

A Fellow of the Royal Geographical Society, Clive is a keen walker, backpacker, cycle tourer and traveller. And when they can't find anyone else, Clive occasionally finds himself leading walking and photographic holidays in Iceland or Norway for David Oswin Expeditions.